GW00703381

CORPORATION
OF LONDON

CITY OF LONDON
FREEMEN'S SCHOOL

150
Anniversary
1854 - 2004

This book has been produced with generous funding from the bequest to the School by the late Stanley Alan Kitchener (Old Freeman).
In June 2004, this enabled the School to give a copy to every current pupil and member of staff to celebrate the School's Sesquicentenary.

...their moment to shine

Reflections on the history of the
City of London Freemen's School
1854-2004

by Patricia Jenkins

ISBN 0 9547523 0 9

Printed by Remous Ltd Milborne Port Dorset
Bound by Richard Harsher Ltd Romsey Hampshire

Edited by Lu Hersey and Richard Owsley, Writers Ltd.
with assistance from David Haywood
Designed by Derek Carmichael
Executive Producer John Keeling FBIPP

Published by The City of London Freemen's School
Ashtead Park Surrey

contents

chapter 1

HOW IT ALL BEGAN

The City of London Freemen's School was founded in 1854, an event that its longest serving (1914-1945) Headmaster, W.W. Parkinson, described as follows:

"When we picture ourselves in England in 1854, without any national system of education, at a time when thousands of children never went to school at all, we can appreciate to the full the motives of our founder, Alderman Warren Stormes Hale. He induced the Corporation to open the Freemen's Orphan School, which was established by an Act of Parliament, 1850 for the Religious and Virtuous Education of the Orphan Children of the City of London."

However, Freemen's School owes its foundation largely to an earlier decision to close down the London Workhouse in Bishopsgate, and in the words of an 1829 Act of Parliament, to "devote the proceeds together with its endowments towards the maintenance of a school for poor and destitute children … and to apprenticing such children to industrious trades."

The London Workhouse
(Guildhall Library. Corporation of London)

The London Workhouse

The City of London was responsible for the relief and employment of poor people in the City. It was governed by the Corporation, consisting of the Lord Mayor, Aldermanic Council and Court of Common Council. Historically, the Aldermen of the City of London met weekly in a supreme court, answerable to the crown. Later the common man had a say in the Court of Common Council, comparable to a town council but still holding allegiance to the Crown.

The City had purchased the London Workhouse in 1703, using it as a house of correction for 'sturdy beggars'. Later it housed vagrant and parish children, but by the beginning of the Nineteenth Century, it had become something of a problem. The poor and homeless avoided it, if they could, by moving to the outskirts of the expanding city. With their departure, the Workhouse fell into gradual disuse and disrepair, hence the decision to close it down and use the proceeds towards a school for poor children.

Arguments in the Court of Common Council

A Board of Governors was set up and in 1830 made a formal request to the Court of Common Council for financial assistance to found a school. The matter was debated at great length, often heatedly and gradually two main bodies of opinion emerged.

The majority of governors held fast to their original intention to found a school for the poor and destitute. This was at a time when schools were desperately needed, as education was mostly reserved for the privileged classes. Yet many members of the Court of Common Council were beginning to discuss a much more ambitious project – the founding of a really first-class school "which might be termed emphatically the High School for the City of London" and which should serve to educate the sons of the citizens of London.

Today we might ask why the poor and destitute children, whose care was the responsibility of the Governors, could not be educated in the High School which council members were eager to found for their own children. But in the early years of the nineteenth century, even to the most enlightened and humane, it was quite inconceivable that poor children should be housed and taught with those from well-to-do families.

Warren Stormes Hale
and the City of London School

Warren Stormes Hale
(Guildhall Library. Corporation of London)

At this time in the early 1830s, Warren Stormes Hale appeared on the scene, and in 1833 was elected Chairman of the City Lands Committee. The Common Council asked this committee to consider founding a Corporation School, and the possibility of linking it with a much earlier bequest. (John Carpenter, Town Clerk of London, who died in 1442, had bequeathed properties to provide for the education and nurture of four poor children at school and university.)

Having a strong personality and a genuine interest in education, Hale's imagination was fired by the idea of a really fine school for the City. Under his leadership and influence, the Committee recommended emphatically that the City should found a school on the "most advanced and generous lines" – which led to the foundation of the City of London School (for boys).

So, for the time being, the Governors of the London Workhouse had failed to persuade the Corporation to join them in founding a school for the poor and destitute. However, the House of Lords ruled that the money from the sale of the London Workhouse could not be used for the new school – and the funds were kept intact. Just as importantly, the idea of a school for the poor and needy had taken root in the minds of the City Corporation, even among those who had seemed least attracted to it.

Warren Stormes Hale
and the Freemen's Orphan School

Once he had successfully launched the City of London School, surprisingly it was Hale who again took up the idea of a school for the poor children of London. Having seemingly killed the idea in 1833, he was now mainly responsible for an 1850 Bill being passed in Parliament enabling the City Corporation to use the London Workhouse funds to found a school for "the maintenance and the religious and virtuous education of orphans of Freemen of the City of London."

The Court of Common Council unanimously elected Hale as Chairman of the Committee responsible for implementing the Act, a post which he filled until he became an Alderman in 1857.

Who were these Freemen?

The studies of Edward Richards (pupil 1921-24) tell us that the granting of freedom was essential to every man who wished to earn a livelihood in trade in London. There was a similar system under the Roman Empire, and under the Normans, there grew up a strong organisation of Guilds, later extended to include almost every trade or handicraft. Until 1835 no man could acquire the freedom of the City without having previously become a freeman of a Guild or Company. The School was designed to cater for the orphaned boys and girls of these men. With low life expectancy for adults, there were likely to be many candidates.

The Freedom

All Lord Mayors, Sheriffs, Aldermen and Liverymen are Freemen of the City of London. The title has a nice ring to it, as it suggests you can come and go as you please. In fact in years gone by, it was not far off that.

The rights included, unofficially, to drive sheep over London Bridge, to go about the City with a drawn sword and, if convicted of a capital offence, to be hanged with a silken rope. Freemen could be married in St Paul's Cathedral, buried in the City and be drunk and disorderly, or relieve themselves in public, without fear of arrest. They could set up a market stall anywhere in the City or dig up turf on Tower Green.

As stated in 'Sheep Over London Bridge' by Caroline Arnold, the only remaining privileges of a Freeman of the City of London today are of a charitable nature. Widows of Freemen may be housed in the Freemen's Almshouses and orphans educated at the City of London Freemen's School.

It is possible to obtain the Freedom of the City in one of three ways; by redemption, by right of patrimony or by right of servitude – all are expected to pay for their Freedom. People of any nationality may apply, and there's a long-standing tradition of admitting women.

Even though a modern-day Freeman of the City of London has no right to all those privileges listed earlier, 1,800 take up freedom each year. The really good news is that all the freedom fees are given to City of London Freemen's School.

chapter 2

SETTING UP THE SCHOOL AT FERNDALE ROAD, BRIXTON

An ideal site for the orphan school was found in Shepherds Lane (later Ferndale Road) Brixton. The land belonged to the City and was next to the London Almshouses, now the City of London Freemen's Almshouses. Surrounded by open fields for three miles, the nearest development was at Clapham Common.

The map, dated 1870, shows the Orphanage and the Almshouses in the centre, just below the railway lines. The area was mostly undeveloped and an ideal place for young children to live.

Map of "leafy Brixton" – Godfey Edition
This map dates from 1870 when Ferndale Road
was still called Shepherds Lane.
(Guildhall Library. Corporation of London)

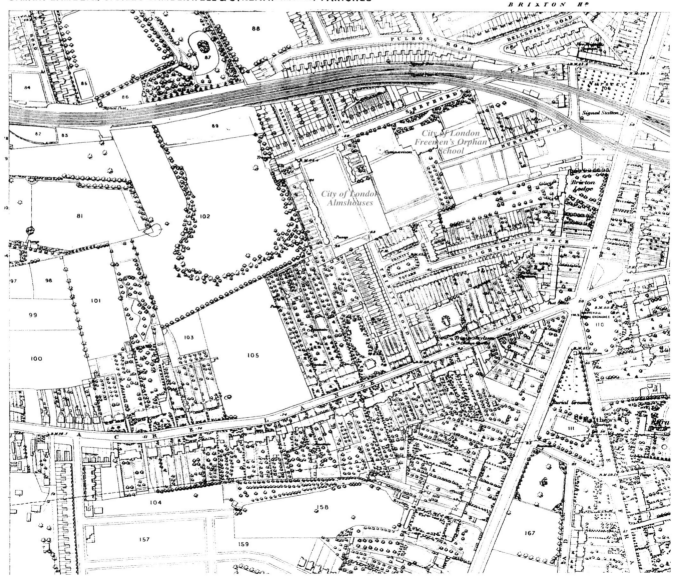

S.ᵗ MARY LAMBETH, S.ᵗ GILES CAMBERWELL & STREATHAM *(Det.)* PARISHES

The Committee responsible for the building of the orphan school first met on 23rd September 1850 and decided:

"It shall be lawful for the (Lord) Mayor, Aldermen and Commons to make and establish such rules and regulations respecting the appointment, number and quality of masters, matrons, teachers and servants to be employed in and about the said School, and their allowance, salaries and wages and the number of children to be from time to time received and educated therein."

A motion to have an equal number of boys and girls was defeated, and they decided on 70 boys and 30 girls. They started planning the accommodation, considered lavish at the time, with two dining rooms, two schoolrooms for the boys and one for the girls. They hoped the money from the sale of the London Workhouse, together with various bequests made for the education of poor children in London, would cover the cost of the building – a total of over £10,000.

The City's Architect started preparing plans for the building. It had to accommodate 100 children, teaching and domestic staff, and provide apartments for the Headmaster and his family. He estimated the building costs at £9,600.

In April 1851 the Committee decided to name the school The City of London Freemen's Orphan School. By October they had received five tenders for the building, varying from nearly £14,000 to almost £16,000. Naturally the Committee chose the lowest, an estimate of £13,707 from a Mr FW Piper, and announced that they would allocate income from certain leases of City owned property to the orphan school.

At last, on 27th April 1852, the Lord Mayor laid the School foundation stone. The distinguished assembly at the ceremony included the Earl of Shaftesbury, the City's representative in Parliament; Sir Edward Buxton, Governor of the Bank of England; and Henry Kemble Esquire, Chairman of the East India Company – something of a celebrity guest list.

Plans of the C.L.F.O.S. – R.E. Everest

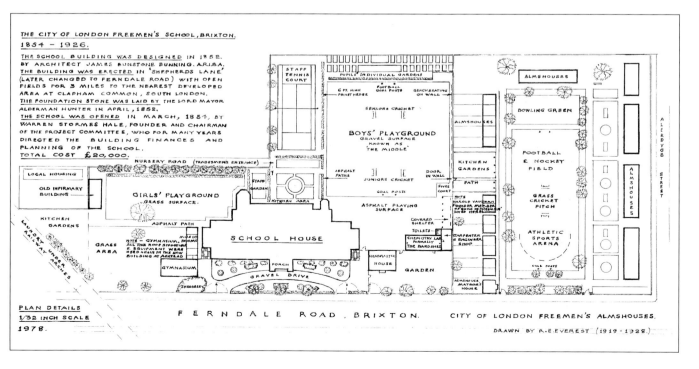

After the foundation stone was laid, the Committee, with Hale as Chairman, continued to oversee the building work and regularly visited the site to inspect progress. They did not wait for the Act of Parliament granting permission for the founding of the City of London Freemen's Orphan School, which was finally passed on 11th January 1853. If they had, the school would never have been completed by 1854.

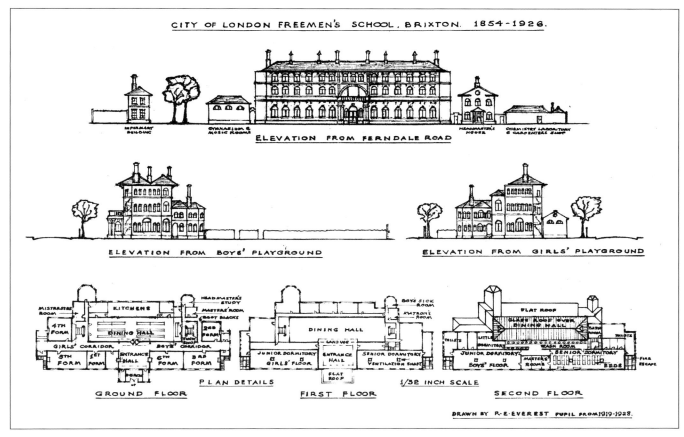

Plans of the C.L.F.O.S. – R.E. Everest

Conditions at the new school were very modern for the time. The Committee received tenders for 'warming apparatus, gas fittings, iron bedsteads, single mattresses of coconut and wool and for laying out the grounds'. Living standards at the school were probably higher than many of the children had previously experienced – even when their fathers were alive.

Finally completed early in 1854, the City of London Freemen's Orphan School was described in contemporary accounts as a handsome and dignified building in red brick and Portland stone and cement, as it seems from the photograph. However, those who actually lived in the orphanage described it as 'grim'.

There were two showpiece features at the School. The first was the splendid entrance hall, but the real pride of the establishment was the large, well-lit dining room. Five carved panels depicted Hogarth's Idle and Industrious Apprentices, for the orphans to meditate on as they ate their meals in silence. The panels were not cheap. Records show an entry of £50 being paid as a part settlement to a Mr John Henning for modelling and fixing them.

Ferndale Road front – Joan Cole

The building had more than enough accommodation for 100 children, and even allowed for expansion. It was very comfortable by the standards of the time, especially considering the living conditions of the poor in London. Only much later did the building come in for criticism, by which time the city had encroached all around and the number of pupils had increased beyond expectation.

Ferndale Road back – Joan Cole

The entrance hall – "1926-1976"

The dining hall – School Archives

chapter 3

THE COMMITTEE TAKES CHARGE

Guidelines for the City of London Freemen's Orphan School

After the foundation stone was laid in 1852, the Committee spent the two years during the building of the school working out how it should be run when it opened. They decided a committee appointed by the City Corporation would manage it.

The School was to provide for orphans who had no means of support and could not afford any education since the death of their fathers. The Committee decided the number of pupils should be "70 boys and 30 girls, to be admitted to the school between the ages of 7 and 10 and to be kept until the age of 14, during which time they should be fed, clothed and educated without charge."

Admission

Applications for admission to the new City of London Freemen's Orphan School had to be sent with the recommendation of at least one member of Common Council. Then, after approval by the Committee, names would be passed to Common Council for election by ballot.

It is clear from the application forms that many families suffered great hardship, and would have been overjoyed at the chance of getting one or two children clothed, fed and educated for free.

Cholera, tuberculosis and other diseases were rife at this time. The loss of the breadwinner, especially if he had suffered a long, drawn-out illness, must have been devastating. Some of the children applying had lost both parents, and their grandparents or other close relatives had completed the forms.

"A Court for King Cholera" from Illustrated English Social History 4 by GM Trevelyan

Learning

A sub-committee, after consultation with Dr Mortimer, Headmaster of the City of London School, drew up the following 'course of instruction':

Boys	Girls
Reading and spelling	Reading and spelling
Writing	Writing
Arithmetic	Arithmetic
English grammar & composition	English grammar & composition
Geography	Geography
History	History
Book-keeping	French
Drawing from models	Drawing
Geometry and Algebra	Music (as far as the Mistress may
French	be able teach it)
Latin	Needlework
Religious Knowledge	Religious Knowledge

This was a surprisingly wide curriculum for 1853, and may have been put forward by Dr Mortimer – though generally the Committee were fiercely independent and not prone to being influenced by outsiders.

Staff

Initially the Committee decided to appoint a Headmaster, a Mistress and a Matron. Resolving "the Master of the Orphan School should be a clergyman of the Church of England at the time of his election and not exceeding 40 years of age," they fixed his salary at £300 a year.

Advertisements for staff were placed in the Times, Mercury, Herald, Chronicle, Advertiser, and Daily News. The Committee also placed notices in the papers telling parents and guardians how to apply for entry to the School and the date selection was taking place.

The Matron

The first Matron, Mrs Pike, was appointed in November 1853. She evidently made a considerable impression on the Committee, as they changed the maximum age from 40 to 45 so that she could take the post.

Mrs Pike proved a good choice – not retiring until 1883 at the ripe old age of 74.

The Porter and his Duties

Next the Committee appointed Samuel Selwood as Porter and decided on his daily duties as:

- To ring Bells at 6am, 6.50am, 6.55am, 8.45am, 8.55am,10.45am, 10.55am,1.45pm,1.55pm, 7pm, 7.55pm.
- To clean Masters' boots, unlock doors, superintend the cleaning of the boys'

boots (morning and evening), clean lavatories, clean knives twice daily, post letters at 12.55pm and 4.55pm.

- To clean Girls' boots.
- To fit Boys with boots and slippers, sending same for repair when necessary.
- To attend to three furnaces.
- To carry coals from cellar for about thirty fires in the winter months.
- To attend to five classroom fires in the winter months.
- To clean Headmaster's school-room.
- To take messages for the Headmaster and Matron.
- To light and put out the gas, and lock up at night.
- To carve at dinner time.

He was also expected, among other incidental duties, to lay carpets, dust the statues and keep an eye on any workmen employed on the premises. His wife was expected to keep the entrance hall clean, and to answer the front door when he was busy. His wages were settled at 21 shillings a week, "with rations (not including beer), two rooms, uniform, and medical attendance, also uniform dress for wife."

He also had to undergo a medical examination before he could start.

The First Headmaster

In the same month the first Headmaster was appointed - the Reverend W. Brownrigg Smith, formerly second Classics Master at the City of London School.

A sensitive, kindly and sympathetic man, he got the School off to a good start – although he set high standards, he managed to win the immediate affection of his pupils. The City of London Freemen's Orphan School was probably a far nicer place to be than most orphanages at the time.

Other Staff

The Committee decided that Mistresses "should not exceed 35 years of age and should have a salary of £40 per annum whilst Matron would earn £60 a year." They appointed Miss Smith as Mistress and Mr Harroway as Assistant Master shortly after the opening of the School.

Daily Regulations

Here is the daily routine decided by the Committee for the new school.

6am	Servants' duties commence – children rise
7	Children down – servants' breakfast
8	Prayers – children's breakfast
9	Studies
10.30	Cessation of study
12 noon	Studies cease – servants' dinner
12.50pm	Children prepare for dinner
1	Children's dinner
2.30	Studies

4.30	Studies cease
5.50	Prepare for supper
6	Supper
7	Oct – Apr Prayers and children retire to rest
8	May – Sept Prayers and children retire to rest
10	Servants retire to rest

Holidays

Holidays were few and short, a fortnight in the summer and a week at Christmas. Visitors were allowed on the first Wednesday of alternate months.

First Elections

Three elections of children took place before the opening date, 28th March 1854.

Typical of those selected were Edward Colbourn, aged nine, and his brother Albert, aged eight, sons of a carcass butcher. With eight children in the Colbourn family, having two of them provided for must have been a great relief to Mrs Colbourn after her husband's death – and many of the orphans came from big families like this. The following table shows the wide variety of jobs the children's fathers held before they died.

We do not have any record of how the first orphans found conditions at the

*List of first elected
(Guildhall Library. Corporation of London)*

GIRLS.

Name.	Born.	Occupation of late Father.	Number of Children left.	Number dependent.	Residence.
1. Eckstein, Elizabeth	5th Jan. 1844	Ironmonger	7	7	1, High street, Notting hill.
2. Matthews, Sarah	14th Apr. 1845	Currier	4	4	7, Lambeth hill.
3. Rolls, Phœbe	14th Jan. 1846	Clerk in an Assurance Office	5	1	Mr. Bailey's, Christ's Hospital.
4. Thies, Clara	19th Aug. 1844	Baker	6	4	61, Old Broad street.
5. Wheeler, Emily	23rd Aug. 1845	Auctioneer	7	5	5, Bury court, St. Mary Axe.
6. Alderson, Mary Elizabeth	12th Aug. 1845	Victualler	4	4	The Woolpack, Hart street.
7. Eden, Angelina Frances Cranfield	21st Mar. 1844	Dentist	3	3	1, Whittaker place, Rye lane, Peckham.
8. Hoar, Martha Ellen	24th Nov. 1845	Timber Merchant	5	5	18, Brownlow road, Dalston.
9. Noble, Emma	12th July, 1844	Bookseller	4	3	2, Emanuel place, St. Giles, Camberwell.
10. Richmond, Matilda	27th Mar. 1845	Plumber, &c.	6	4	18, Whitefriars street, Fleet street.
11. Bishop, Julia Susannah Corbould	23rd Aug. 1844	Upholsterer	1	1	40, Newington place, Kennington.
12. Faver, Marianne	18th Feb. 1845	Oil and Colourman	3	2	2, Rosetta place, Coburg road, Old Kent road.
13. Kislingbury, Edith	26th Nov. 1846	Wine Merchant	7	5	16, Medina villas, Dalston lane.
14. Rogers, Elizabeth	11th May, 1846	Victualler	2	2	3, Mayo place, Camberwell lane, Brixton.
15. Scrivener, Catherine	11th Sept. 1844	Compositor	5	4	4, Stepney causeway.
16. Smith, Susannah	15th Apr. 1845	Lighterman	6	5	3, Great Cherry Garden street, Bermondsey.
17. Walls, Henrietta Frances	2nd Nov. 1846	Tailor	5	3	4, Sidney street, Commercial road.
18. Walters, Charlotte	2nd June, 1844	Tobacconist	3	3	10, King street, Kingsland.

LIST OF CHILDREN ELECTED

Up to 28th March, 1854.

BOYS.

Name.	Born.	Occupation of late Father.	Number of Children left.	Number dependent.	Residence.
1. Colbourn, Edward	20th Mar. 1845	Carcase Butcher	8	6	1, Swan street, Minories.
2. Grierson, David Holt	18th Feb. 1846	Vellum Binder	6	2	2, Hare row, Cambridge heath.
3. Jones, John	12th July, 1844	Grocer	4	4	18, Ampthill square, Hampstead road.
4. Kislingbury, Arthur	3rd May, 1845	Wine Merchant	7	6	16, Medina villas, Dalston.
5. Miles, Walter Brooks	13th Sept. 1844	Surgeon, &c.	6	6	5, Lilford road, Camberwell.
6. Vohman, George Henry	19th Sept. 1845	Baker	4	4	4, Broadway, Blackfriars.
7. Volckman, George Frederic	15th Aug. 1844	Calenderer	3	3	11, Daggett's court, Finsbury.
8. Vousden, William	25th Feb. 1844	Stonemason	4	3	High street, Clapham.
9. Akam, Walter Frederick	1st Oct. 1844	Shoemaker	5	5	91, Bunhill row.
10. Brigham, Robert.	31st Dec. 1845	Livery-Stable Keeper	7	5	14, Cowper street, City road.
11. Colbourn, Albert.	15th Nov. 1846	Carcase Butcher.	8	6	1, Swan street, Minories.
12. Daniel, Edward Gordon	14th Mar. 1846	Fruiterer, &c.	7	7	2, Bull-head pas., Gracechurch st.
13. Daniel, Herbert Cato	21st Dec. 1846	Upholsterer	5	5	1, Frederick place, Brixton hill.
14. Eckstein, William	10th Mar. 1846	Ironmonger	7	5	1, High street, Notting hill.
15. Groves, William	8th Jan. 1845	Greengrocer	3	2	30, Poppin's court, Fleet street.

Name.	Born.	Occupation of late Father.	Number of Children left.	Number dependent.	Residence.
16. Hood, Frederick John	1st Feb. 1844	Carver and Gilder	3	2	16, Singleton street, Hoxton.
17. Kipling, William Nicholas	15th May, 1845	Manchester Ware-houseman	2	2	7, Whatfort street, St. Pancras.
18. Ledger, Benjamin	23rd July, 1846	Wool Broker.	1	1	9, Enfield road North, West Hackney.
19. Reffell, Henry Waghorn	12th Feb. 1844	Lighterman	5	4	12, Charles street, Hatton garden.
20. Walker, Benjamin	18th July, 1845	Goldbeater	8	3	41, Gray's-inn-lane, Holborn.
21. Anderson, Duncan	28th Jan. 1847	Chemist, &c.	2	2	Bromsgrove house, Stockwell green.
22. Crossthwaite William Eugène	30th Jan. 1847	Merchant	3	3	13, Park villas, Hammersmith.
23. Davies, George Edward	10th July, 1845	Coal Merchant	9	4	41, Ewer st. Union st. Southwark.
24. Hood, George James	5th Dec. 1846	Carver and Gilder	1	1	16, Singleton street, Hoxton.
25. Morley, Joseph George	31st Jan. 1847	Piano and Music Seller	3	3	10, Stockwell ter. Clapham road.
26. Welch, Edward Alfred	19th Dec. 1846	Clerk in General Post Office	8	6	9, Huntingdon street, Barnsbury.
27. Zabell, Frederic William	22nd Sept.1845	Sugar Baker	4	4	25, Durham st. Hackney road.
28. Atkins, John Edward	17th July, 1845	Undertaker	7	6	13, Church street, Spitalfields.
29. Birch, William Walter	8th Sept. 1845	Poultry Salesman, &c.	5	5	2, Ashmole cottage, Church street, Kennington.
30. Hankins, Thomas	4th Mar. 1846	Wine Merchant	1	1	3, Norman's buildings, St. Luke's.
31. Richmond, George	26th Feb. 1847	Plumber, &c.	6	3	18, Whitefriars street, Fleet street.
32. Webster, Stephen	4th Mar. 1846	Farrier and Veterinary Surgeon	5	3	6, Upper John street, White-horse lane, Stepney.

List of first elected
(Guildhall Library. Corporation of London)

school, but later in the book there are plenty of recollections of children who went to Brixton around the turn of the century. It must have been very daunting to young, bereaved children when they first arrived, but most of them grew to appreciate the opportunities the school gave them in life. As Daisy Wiard (left in 1928) later recalled: "Although adversity catapulted us, at a very young age, into a daunting but caring boarding school world, the education and training provided there instilled hope and courage to face the future with confidence and a grateful appreciation for all the happy memories."

The Official Opening

We know from the City archives that the Lord Mayor and a large section of the Court of Common Council went to Brixton for the school opening. The Lord Mayor, Chairman Warren Stormes Hale and Dr Mortimer, Headmaster of the City of London School, all gave speeches, followed by a prayer and blessing on the School from the Headmaster, Brownrigg Smith. After a conducted tour of the building, every child was presented with a new shilling.

Early Days

Teaching must have been hard work in the early years at the School, as many of the children admitted could neither read nor write. This is not surprising, as at the time the church, or other charitable foundations provided the only education available to most people.

There were also very few staff and many subjects to cover – and no question of sorting out children according to their age or ability. With only two classes, boys and girls were taught separately, and kept strictly apart for the whole day. In fact they were only housed under the same roof because it was an orphanage. Though considered undesirable, it was much cheaper.

Of course, despite segregation, older children found ways of getting round the rules. Old Freemen later told many tales of clandestine meetings and note-passing between boys and girls.

The Role of the Committee

The Committee played an extremely active part in running the School, deciding on everything from curriculum to diet. They gave the Headmaster instructions to buy books of "an instructive character for the children to read out of school hours" and even told him which books to buy. And woe betide him if he did anything without first consulting them. In his first two years Brownrigg Smith was rebuked three times by the Committee: for introducing a Latin grammar piece he had composed himself; for arranging a 'geographical' lecture; and for arranging extra pews at church to accommodate the growing numbers of scholars in the School.

Food

The children were very well fed and probably had not had such a good diet in their own homes. Food for each meal was entirely decided and set down by the Committee as follows:

BREAKFAST

Not less than 6ozs. of bread and half a pint of new milk for each child

DINNER

Sunday	Cold baked beef with potatoes
Monday	Batter pudding with meat (alternately)
	Cold meat with bread and baked rice pudding
Tuesday	Boiled leg of mutton with potatoes, vegetables or rice and bread
Wednesday	Soup thickened with rice and bread and plum pudding
Thursday	Baked beef with potatoes or greens and bread
Friday	Stewed beef with boiled rice and bread
Saturday	Baked leg of mutton with potatoes or rice and bread

SUPPER

Bread and cheese, butter or treacle (not less than 6ozs. of bread per child) and a pint of milk and water.

Grace

Before and after every meal, the children always said grace. Len Voller
(who attended the School 1913-1922) sent this amusing observation:

BENEDICTUS BENEDECAT PER JESUM CHRISTUM
DOMINUM NOSTRUM, AMEN

At school, when at meals we met	
Before and after each was said…..	
So three meals a day	6 times
A week of seven days, yes,	
We also ate on Sundays!	42 times
Twelve weeks a term	504 times
Three terms a year	1512 times
For nine years and two terms,	
So I must have heard it, ere	
My school days ceased, about	13,500 times
At least!	

The Conder Prize

Within a few years, progress at the City of London Freemen's Orphan School began to impress people in the City. In 1860, Edward Conder, citizen and wheelwright of London, decided to donate a Testimonial Fund he had been awarded in recognition of his services as an Alderman. He arranged to have the

Prize Day – School Archives

Fund, which was about £5 a year, given to the School instead. He wanted it to be used to provide an annual prize for 'a deserving scholar' when they left school. Soon there were a plethora of annual prizes to award at Prize Day, thanks to donations from Freemen of the City.

Sickness and Health

Some of the medical treatment the children received would be considered extraordinary today. The Committee made provision for bottles of port to be supplied for the use of sick children 'under the direction of the Surgeon'. They also arranged 'the supply of Guinness draught Stout for the use of convalescent and other children as may be necessary.'

Although the Governors of the School demanded a health certificate before any child could be accepted, it was at a time when many illnesses could not be cured, and sadly it was not uncommon for children to die when epidemics swept through the school.

Exams

The children all sat exams every year, overseen by an external examiner, to show they were making reasonable progress. The following is a portion of an Algebra exam from 1864.

Results were not entirely unbiased. The examiner was anxious to retain his fees for a relatively easy job, and tended to err on the favourable side.

CITY OF LONDON FREEMEN'S ORPHAN SCHOOL.

ANNUAL EXAMINATION, 1864.

ALGEBRA.

1. If $a = 7$ $b = 1$ $c = 10$ $x = 4$ $y = 5$.
   Find the value of $10\,a - 10\,b + c$.
   of $a + 3\,b - c$.
   of $\dfrac{a^2\,x^2 + b^2\,y^2 + c^2}{6\,abc}$.

2. Add together $3\,a + 2\,b - c$; $4\,a - 5\,b + 3\,c$; $5\,a + b - 5\,c$.
   Add together $x + y$; $-3\,x + 7\,y$; $4\,x - 7\,y$.
   Add together $7\,a - 3\,b + 10$; $-8\,a + 4\,b - 11$; $12\,a - 14$; $-a - b - 1$.
   Subtract $a - b - c$ from $a + b + c$.
   Subtract $3\,a^3 - 5\,a^2\,x - 3\,ax^2 - 3\,x^3$ from $5\,a^3 - 4\,a^2\,x + 2\,ax^2 - 3\,x^3$.

3. Multiply $3\,a^2 - 5\,ab + 2\,b^2$ by $4\,a$.
   $x^2 + 3\,x + 2$ by $x - 3$.
   $3\,a^2 - 5\,ab + 2\,b^2$ by $a^2 - 7\,ab$.
   $a^2 - ab + b^2$ by $a - b$.
   $a^3 + 2\,a^2\,b + 2\,ab^2 + b^3$ by $a^3 - 2\,a^2\,b + 2\,ab^2 - b^3$.

Further education

School and City archives show that although pupils had to leave the City of London Freemen's School on their fifteenth birthday, any highly gifted children were given further support and encouragement, sometimes staying on as 'pupil teachers'.

It was even possible for exceptionally talented orphan children to continue their education as far as university or college, with the Committee helping them find grants and bursaries to see them through financially. One such boy, Harry George Cole, entered the City of London Freemen's Orphan School in 1860, already aged eight and unable to read or write. Staff soon realised he had an aptitude for learning, especially mathematics, and he received extra tuition from the Headmaster to encourage him. He went on to win every possible prize during his school career.

When it was time for him to leave at the age of fifteen, the School encouraged him to continue his studies. Helped by grants from the City, Harry eventually went up to Cambridge University. This was a significant achievement for a poor orphan child a century and a half ago – though tragically Harry died soon after getting his degree of some ailment that 'first attacked the brain and ultimately terminated fatally in rapid consumption', most probably something easily curable today. But Harry's story still demonstrates how good the education at the City of London Freemen's Orphan School could be.

chapter 4

THE SECOND HEADMASTER

Marcus Tulloch Cormack, 1866–1889

After the sad death of the first Headmaster, Brownrigg Smith, in 1866, he was paid this tribute by the External Examiner, the Rev W Webster, Fellow of Queen's College, Cambridge: "Few have been so richly endowed by nature in the combination of intellectual power with the more attractive graces of sympathy, sweetness and love. The mildness of his disposition and the gentleness of his manner, tempered with firmness and regulated by discretion, had an influence on the minds of his pupils which is not likely to be effaced."

Marcus Tulloch Cormack succeeded him and held the post until 1889.

Increasing numbers of staff and pupils

By 1869 the number of pupils had risen to one hundred and fifty. Staff numbers also rose. By the1880s there was a Headmaster, three Assistant Masters, a Headmistress, two Assistant Mistresses, four part time teachers, a Drill Sergeant and a Band Master. We are fortunate to have the following two accounts from former pupils attending the school during Cormack's time as Headmaster.

T.J. Aucock was a pupil from 1865–1872. In 1954, at the School's centenary, he was asked to comment on his time as a pupil. He was ninety-seven at the time.

"I entered the Freemen's School, which was then in Brixton, when I was eight years old and left on my fifteenth birthday, 6th March 1872. At that time the School was only for the orphans of City of London Freemen, and that was why my sister and I went there.

There were 100 boys and 50 girls. The boys wore grey knickerbocker suits and Inverness capes. I can't remember how the girls were dressed but they had to wear their hair in ringlets – and I remember the girls did the boys' mending in their needlework lessons.

There were not any houses between our School and Clapham Common, as Brixton was then in the country. The Headmaster was a fine type of Scotsman named Mr Cormack; Second Master Mr Harroway and third Mr Boswell. Our drawing Master was Mr Dicksee, brother of the famous painter of that name.

We were all boarders then. The School was a very fine building with a handsome entrance hall with statuettes leading to the dining hall, lit by a glass roof, and all around the walls were carvings of the Idle and Industrious Apprentices by Hogarth. At the top of the staircase leading out of there was a large statue of Dick Whittington listening to Bow Bells.

Our day started with a basin of milk each, our bread being weighed for us. In fact all our food was weighed and the amount we got depended on our age.

The dormitories were on the top floor with forty beds in each and twenty young boys slept on the lower floor. In my last year I was in charge of them - each dormitory had a monitor in charge.

We played football and cricket and did gymnastics. I remember we were playing football one day when our Headmaster joined in, and accidentally fell on the ball. He flattened it out completely – but being a good sport, he paid for a new one.

Another thing I remember very well is going with other boys and girls to see Blackfriars Bridge opened by Queen Victoria, and seeing her knight the Lord Mayor afterwards.

Very handsome prizes were given in those days and I still have a number of them. They were always presented by the Lord Mayor of London. Ironically I was being kept in for misbehaviour when I was told I had won the coveted Scripture prize."

A very faded photograph of the girls at Brixton – Joan Cole

John W. Cookson, a pupil at the school from1885-1890, gave this account in 1950.

"I left in 1890 and can still recollect many things that happened in my five years at the School. My box of school mementos includes these two photos, one of the boys and the other of the girls in our own playgrounds.

I've also got my bronze medal with Queen Victoria on one side and the City Coat of Arms on the reverse, which we were given to commemorate her Jubilee, 1837-1887. I recollect we had bread and treacle for tea that day.

Our Headmaster was Mr Cormack, and when he left, Mr Montague. His assistants were Mr Harroway, Mr Boswell, Mr Stephenson, and Mr Barnes, with Mrs Woolridge as the Matron.

As I have said many times I am proud of the School. I was apprenticed from the Guildhall, served my seven years, and never been out of work for one minute from the day I started until I retired about two years ago."

A very faded photograph of the boys at Brixton – Joan Cole

The troubles of 1889

Cormack's time as Headmaster came to an end in 1889. That year there were a number of problems with the boys and discipline broke down completely. Boys were breaking out and also playing truant. There was also deliberate vandalism and teachers' authority was openly defied.

The trouble stemmed from the previous year when an epidemic had swept the building. Sometimes more than fifty boys at a time had been confined to sick quarters, and it was almost impossible to maintain constant supervision and control.

Things got so bad that Cormack and some members of staff eventually felt obliged to offer their resignations. The Governors reluctantly accepted, despite the long and honourable service they had all given the School. They also suspended twelve senior boys, including a 'pupil teacher', for five months. Most of the suspended boys would have left by the end of the five months anyway, once they had turned fifteen – but it was a sad end to Cormack's career as Headmaster.

chapter 5

1890 TO END OF 19TH CENTURY

New staff and new ideas

Following the troubles in 1889, RE Montague was appointed Headmaster. He quickly restored order, and life at the City of London Freemen's Orphan School went back to normal. He was joined by three other outstanding members of staff, all of whom stayed on at the School for most of their working lives – Miss Robins, Mr Lowe and Mr Roberts. Their pupils remembered them all with affection in later years.

Montague kept the children well occupied to keep them out of any further trouble, as we can see from some samples of his timetables on page 27.

He made one very important innovation during his time as Headmaster, which was entering pupils for the Cambridge Junior Examination. Up to then, a visiting examiner commissioned by the Committee was the only person to assess pupils' work. Working on an annual fee basis, to retain the work his reports tended to be favourable. You can see copies of these reports in the City Archives at the Guildhall.

By 1894, the Committee were so pleased with the way Montague was running the School, they sought permission from the Court of Common Council to increase the number of pupils to 100 boys and 65 girls. By 1895 the school roll was up to 163.

In 1898 the Committee decided that the 'Housekeeper' should become the 'Matron', and the new post was advertised with the following job description:

Mr Lowe – T. Riley

Duties of the Matron

To be performed under the control and supervision of the Headmaster

Mr Roberts – T. Riley

- To superintend and manage the domestic affairs of the Institution.

- To take, when required, general charge of the School establishment and children during the holidays appointed by the Committee.

- To receive all furniture, clothing and other requisites, weigh and inspect all articles of food, &c., check all invoices, and keep a daily account thereof in a book, to be submitted to the Headmaster when required, and laid before the monthly meeting of the Sub-Committee at the School.

- To be responsible for the cleanliness of the School premises, the making (except the outer garments of the boys) and repair, as also the cleanliness of the linen and apparel of both Boys and Girls.

- To provide all children's meals agreeably to the dietary, which is to be strictly observed.

- To provide suitable meals for the Officers and Servants.

- To have the care of invalid children, Boys and Girls, under the directions of the Medical Officer.

- To have control of the female servants.

- To keep a Diary of Occurrences, to be laid before the Committee, Sub-Committee, or the Headmaster, when required.

- To report to the Committee any dereliction of duty of any of the female servants of the Institution.

- To give all orders to the appointed tradesmen.

- To see that all doors are safely fastened for the night, and that all the inmates retire to rest at the appointed time.

- To carry into effect all such orders and directions as may from time to time be given by the Committee.

Candidates must be either widows without encumbrance, or single. The age must be not under 30, nor over 45 years at the time of election. Salary £60 per annum, with Bed Room and Sitting Room, Board, Fuel, Light, Washing, and Medical Attendance.

An Old Boy's Tale – recollections from the turn of the century

Harold Victor Smith – from a letter written by his daughter.

"My father died on 27th January 1971, at the age of 85. He left the City of London Freemen's Orphan School, as it was then called, on 16th June 1900, and a few days later, aged 15, became a member of the staff of the Corporation of London at Guildhall where he remained for 45 years until his retirement. He was at the old School at Brixton, and as children, my sisters and I loved to hear stories about 'The Orphan School' as he called it – like how many pairs of boots he had to clean before breakfast. A really thick slice of bread has always been known in our house as an 'Orphan School slice'.

He retained his interest in the School to the end of his life and last went to an Old Freemen's Day in June 1969 – in fact he was so keen not to miss it (and by then rather forgetful) that he went to Ashtead on the Wednesday before the Saturday and was given tea by the School. He enjoyed this much more than the following Saturday when he went to Ashtead again for the proper occasion and was lost in the crowds."

This letter was originally printed in "Ashteadian" number 83.

CITY OF LONDON FREEMEN'S ORPHAN SCHOOL, BRIXTON, S.W.

TIME TABLE.
GIRLS.

Vertical divider columns: 8.0 = BREAKFAST · 9.0 = PRAYERS · 10.45 = RECREATION · 12.40 = DINNER · 5.30 = TEA · 7.0 = PREPARATION CLASS · 8.0 = PRAYERS

Time	Class	9.10	10	11.0	11.30	12.0	2.0	2.30	3.30
Monday	1	Arithmetic	Scripture	Needle	work	Singing	Dictation	Drawing	Knitting
	2	Arithmetic	Scripture	Grammar	Spelling	Singing	Dictation	Needlework	Reading
	3	Arithmetic	Scripture	Geography	Spelling	Singing	Needle	work	Reading
Tuesday	1	Arithmetic	Grammar	Harmony	Geography	Writing	Needle	work	Drill
	2	Arithmetic	Obj. Lesson	Needle	work	Writing	Geography	Composition	Drill
	3	Arithmetic	Obj. Lesson	History	Dictation	Reading	Writing	Spelling	Drill
Wednesday	1	French	M. Arithmetic	History	German	Composition	HALF-HOLIDAY		
	2	Arithmetic	French	History	Spelling	Dictation	HALF-HOLIDAY		
	3	Arithmetic	Grammar	French	Needle	work	HALF-HOLIDAY		
Thursday	1	Arithmetic	Scripture	Needle	work	Singing	O. T. Hist.	Drawing	Knitting
	2	Arithmetic	Scripture	Gram	mar	Singing	Dictation	Needlework	Reading
	3	Arithmetic	Scripture	Geography	Spelling	Singing	Needle	work	Reading
Friday	1	Arithmetic	Grammar	Harmony	Geography	Writing	Needle	work	Drill
	2	Arithmetic	Reading	Needle	work	Writing	Geography	Dictation	Drill
	3	Arithmetic	Reading	History	Dictation	Spelling	Writing	Grammar	Drill
Saturday	1	German	Arithmetic	History	French	Dictation	HALF-HOLIDAY		
	2	Arithmetic	French	History	Spelling	Writing	HALF-HOLIDAY		
	3	Arithmetic	Grammar	French	Needle	work	HALF-HOLIDAY		

Boys and Girls Timetables (Guildhall Library. Corporation of London)

N.B.—Each girl has, in addition to the above instruction, half-an-hour's music lesson and half-an-hour's practice each week.

TIME TABLE.
BOYS.

Vertical divider columns: 8.0 = BREAKFAST · 9.0 = PRAYERS · 10.45 = RECREATION · 12.40 = DINNER · 5.30 = TEA · 7.0 = PREPARATION CLASS · 8.0 = PRAYERS

Time	Class	9.10	9.45	10.0	10.15	11.0	11.30	12.0	2.0	3.0	3.30
Monday	1	Arithmetic	French			Grammar	Composition	Shorthand	Drawing	Singing	Drill
	2	Arithmetic		Scripture		French		Latin	Drawing	Reading	Drill
	3	French	Arithmetic		Reading	Grammar	Spelling	Writing	Drawing	Reading	Drill
Tuesday	1	Arithmetic	German			Algebra	History	Shorthand	Book-keeping	Latin	Science
	2	Arithmetic		Geography		French		Latin	Ment. Arith.	Grammar	Singing
	3	French	Arithmetic		Reading	History	Spelling	Dictation	Arithmetic	Writing	Reading
Wednesday	1	Arithmetic	Latin			Euclid	Geography	Shorthand	HALF-HOLIDAY		
	2	Euclid	Arithmetic		History	Writing	Dictation	Latin	HALF-HOLIDAY		
	3	Arithmetic		Reading		Geography	Writing	Singing	HALF-HOLIDAY		
Thursday	1	Arithmetic	French			Grammar	Composition	Shorthand	Drawing	Singing	Drill
	2	Arithmetic		Scripture		French		Latin	Drawing	Reading	Drill
	3	French	Arithmetic		Reading	Grammar	Spelling	Dictation	Drawing	Spelling	Drill
Friday	1	Arithmetic	German			Algebra	History	Shorthand	Scripture	Latin	Science
	2	Arithmetic		Grammar		French		Latin	Writing	Geography	Singing
	3	French	Arithmetic		Reading	History	Writing	Spelling	Scripture	Dictation	Reading
Saturday	1	Arithmetic	Latin			Euclid	Geography	Shorthand	HALF-HOLIDAY		
	2	Euclid	Arithmetic		History	Writing	Dictation	Latin	HALF-HOLIDAY		
	3	Arithmetic		Reading		Geography	Writing	Singing	HALF-HOLIDAY		

R. E. MONTAGUE, M.A.,
Head Master.

chapter 6

EARLY 20TH CENTURY

Overcrowding and Poor Health

By the end of the Nineteenth Century, Brixton had become engulfed by the rapid expansion of London. There were no longer open spaces for the children to play in, and life at Ferndale Road was becoming more and more restricted. Worse, the children's health was affected and a number of serious epidemics broke out. Parties of children were regularly sent to the seaside for a change of air and the school often closed before the end of term to prevent disease spreading.

In November 1899, the Minister of Health for the Parish of Lambeth wrote to the Committee noting there had been three cases of diphtheria and 'much illness among the inmates during the past year'. The Minister recommended the School be closed immediately, and considered 'the sanitary arrangements altogether behind modern requirements'. The Committee decided to move everyone to temporary accommodation in Norfolk while the essential alterations were made to the School.

They moved back in April 1900 when the building work was complete, but with strict orders from the Minister not to allow overcrowding to recur. The Committee resolved to start searching for potential sites to build a new school, to re-house the pupils and possibly expand their numbers. Various options were considered over the following year, but unfortunately proved too expensive to be viable.

In just one term in 1900, the School doctor reported there had been 93 children in the infirmary and he had made a further 161 visits to see pupils with minor ailments. Things were getting serious.

Meanwhile, various events in the City also had long term repercussions for the Orphanage. The formation of the City Imperial Volunteers, a force of volunteers for the war in South Africa, was underway. Because of their origins in the City, and the funding donated by the Common Council, the Volunteers all received the freedom of the City before leaving for war. And because the men had been given the freedom of the City, the children of those who died in conflict were eligible for acceptance into the Orphanage – which meant numbers of pupils continued to rise. Sooner or later the Committee would have to find new premises for the school.

Recollections of School pupils from the turn of the century

For the time being, however, life at the Orphanage carried on as usual and the pupils were oblivious to any long-term problems the School may be encountering. The following recollections from students living there at the turn of the century provide an interesting insight to the way of life at the old school.

Miss C. M. Gaisford (1899–1904)

"My time at Brixton covers the years 1899 to 1902, with a further extension to 1904, when I was allowed to stay on while attending the City of London School for Girls.

By modern standards, you might regard the life then as somewhat austere, but it was a happy, wholesome one, in the course of which we received a sound education.

The building was a solid structure standing in its own grounds. Separate from the main building was the Infirmary, a little house, where sick children received special care. Adjoining the School were the Almshouse grounds and it was here in the grassy, tree-shadowed quadrangle that we spent the long summer evening of Prize Day.

One feature that strikes me, in retrospect, as a little unusual, was the plaster-cast groupings, life-size, that stood out in relief from the upper part of the dining room walls, with here and there a suitable text, like 'The fear of the Lord is the beginning of Wisdom.' Since talking wasn't allowed during mealtimes, we had plenty of time to ponder over them.

With the general use of gas, a fire escape was essential. Ours was a strong, canvas tubular affair, attached to the dormitory window, ready to be thrown to the playground below. Going down it in record time was a breathtaking experience, quite a diversion from the ordinary routine, especially on a dark evening!

The person I remember with most affection was Miss Robins. Through her we gained a love of Kipling, and everything connected with India, and she was always so interested when we returned as ex-pupils. And so was Sarah, the maid responsible for our clothes. I can see her now in her starched linen dress, a delightful character from days gone by.

With the Cambridge Junior Examination in view, we were kept well occupied. It was about this time that Shorthand and Typing took the place of German, as girls were taking up clerical work on leaving School.

Apart from a memorable visit to the Guildhall, I can recall only two outings, one to Wateringbury by River, and another to hear Ben Davies sing. We were not in the habit of looking beyond the School for our amusements. In the summer there was tennis, the highlight being the contest for the Novice's and Veteran's racquets. Then too, we had a well-chosen library. All things considered, life seemed to go on in a serene, orderly way from day to day.

As a child one accepts priceless benefits, as the birds take the berries from the hedge-rows – but looking back on school life, I appreciate its more spiritual values, and realise to the full the debt I owe to the Freemen of the City of London."

Miss Edith Keene (left 1905)

"The School building was quite large, for we were to some extent a self-contained community. The recreation grounds were at the back of the School, and well away from the main building were the Infirmary and the Laundry. The Headmaster's house and garden were next to the School, and then came the Gresham and City Almshouses with their own grounds. It was on the long green in these grounds that the girls played hockey, and on Prize Days gave a drill display. The tennis court was in our own grounds.

Discipline was very strict, but that was not unusual in those days. It would probably seem incredible to modern children that so much silence was imposed upon us.

At this time, around the turn of the century, the number of boys was about 85 and the number of girls about 60.

The School Routine

Unlike today, we did not just have schoolwork for a certain number of hours and then our own free time. Once the day had started at 7am (except in winter), we went to our classrooms for three quarters of an hour preparation, then the whole day was mapped out by time-tables and lists of duties.

Breakfast was in the Dining Hall just before eight o'clock, and the Master on duty said grace, in Latin, before and after meals. After breakfast there was a little free time out of doors until the first bell at 8.45, when we were lined up by 8.55 ready to go into the Dining Hall for Prayers. Everyone available was expected to be there: teaching staff, Matron, Nurse and household staff.

Lessons started immediately afterwards, and went on until 12.30 with only a short break, then continued in the afternoon, except on Wednesdays and Saturdays. If it was fine on those afternoons we usually went for a walk in a crocodile formation.

Piano practice started at 7.15am in various rooms and went on at available times during the day. Some years later, soundproof cubicles were built. Usually practice time was half an hour each day, but for those taking the Associated Board R.A.M. and R.M.C. School examinations it was an hour at least, usually two. The two Seniors in Music had to play a duet on Prize Day.

Subjects taught along with reading, writing and arithmetic were history, geography, grammar, scripture, composition, harmony, drawing (freehand and metrical), needlework, french, (Shakespeare came in somewhere), shorthand and typing, and drill by visiting instructors.

On the two long walls of the Dining Hall were plaster casts of the 'Good and Bad Apprentice' by Hogarth, with what were evidently considered appropriate texts from the Bible. In the Committee Room was a large painting of the founder, Warren Stormes Hale. In 1904 we celebrated the 50th year of the School and we received a small medallion with the City Coat of Arms.

We did evening preparation from six o'clock to seven o'clock. Then we had a mug of milk and two very hard biscuits, and the younger children went to bed. The fifth and sixth forms had to study for another hour after Prayers.

Three senior girls were Monitresses and had various duties such as being in charge of Preparation (for no talking was allowed), sitting at the head of a table in the Dining Hall, and being in charge of a dormitory.

Prize Day

Prize Day was a great event, and flags went up in the entrance porch for the arrival of the Lord Mayor in State. The Dining Hall was cleared of tables, and seats arranged for the members of the School Committee and their wives, and other visitors. Deputy Sayer and his wife always came, although getting old, and they seemed to belong to an era of graciousness in their dress, interest and courtesy. Tiers of seats were erected at the end of the hall for us, and we all dressed in our Sunday best. It was also the custom for the sixth form girls to wear a white camellia on our dark blue dresses.

Two girls played a duet, and the girls had to sing, but I do not remember the boys having to do anything. Members of the Common Council, in their gowns,

Lord Mayor Arriving – School Archives

Hall on Prize day – School Archives

received the Lord Mayor in the Entrance Hall, and two girls were in the corridor ready to present bouquets, one to the Lady Mayoress and the other to the Chairman's wife. The Lord Mayor then walked the length of the Hall to the platform, and the prize giving began.

A marquee was erected for the Lord Mayor and the visitors and we had a special Band in the grounds. The Lord Mayor left in his horse-drawn carriage and the girls gave a Drill display accompanied by the Band in the Almshouse gardens. The visitors departed and Prize Day was over, except this was the one occasion fifth and sixth form boys and girls were allowed to mix and talk together for about an hour in the Almshouse grounds. By the next morning the Dining Hall would be back to normal. The next big event would be going home for the summer holiday."

C.M. Gray (pupil 1902–11)

Then and now

"You only have to compare the stony and enforced silence of the dining hall at Brixton, where the boys and girls were segregated at opposite ends – and even that was the only time they ever saw each other – with the cheerful hubbub of the present mixed assembly at their meals.

Even our playgrounds were separated by a kitchen garden, railed in and screened by hedges. This garden was out of bounds and I remember being pushed into this area and threatened by older boys with all kinds of torture if I attempted to come out.

Fire drill

But fire drill was more fun before iron ladders replaced the canvas chute we used to make the descent to safety. We had an accident once during fire drill practice, when a metal tip on a boy's boot was loose and ripped a hole in the canvas. The next boy, who had entered the chute before the rip was noticed, fell straight through. Fortunately the Drill Sergeant ran forward and caught him in his arms. Although the boy was unhurt, he had to be excused fire drill from then on.

Daily routine

If you find the present routine of the Boarding House rigorous, think about the daily routine of the School at Brixton. We all got up at 6.30am, except those unfortunates detailed for bed-making and boot-blacking who got up at 6.00am. We had a wash in cold water, followed by forty-five minutes' prep, before we even had breakfast.

Sundays were very dull days when no games were permitted. The first part of the morning was confined to walking round the playground in our Sunday best, followed by church. In the afternoon we were marched up to Brockwell Park, where we were dismissed and allowed to meet our relatives.

The Band

The School Band, which you do not have any more, was very important at Brixton. We performed on ceremonial occasions, welcoming the Lord Mayor and Sheriffs on Prize Day with the March from 'Scipio.' We also entertained members of the Committee while they dined. On one sad occasion the Head Boy's solo from 'The Chocolate Soldier' turned out disastrously because his cornet had been dropped by the Headmaster.

The Prefects' Book

You might also be interested to learn the origin of the Prefects' Book. Each Monitor (now called a Prefect) had a small notebook where they wrote the names of any offenders. Then from these books the 'bootblacks' and the 'bed makers' were chosen for the week."

chapter 7

A NEW HEADMASTER AND THE OUT BREAK OF THE FIRST WORLD WAR

The Governors were still debating the future of the School and its possible relocation, when the Great War broke out. All plans had to be shelved immediately – not just because there were Zeppelin raids to contend with. Conscription reduced the male teaching staff to the Head and one Assistant Master.

The Arrival of Parkinson

In 1914, W.W. Parkinson was appointed as the new Headmaster. Considered a man ahead of his time, he led the School for thirty-one years and introduced many changes, including the House system and co-educational teaching.

Parkinson's own recollections of starting at the City of London Freemen's Orphan School

"I first saw the inside of the Freemen's Orphan School, Brixton on 25th June 1914, after my election as Headmaster by the Court of Common Council. I was shown over the grim-looking building by R.E. Montague, my predecessor. The Headmaster's House was close to the School and next door were the Freemen's Almshouses, surrounding a grass plot on which the boys and girls played games.

When July came, with the shadow of war in Europe becoming darker, I started for a holiday at the end of the summer term, but after the hostilities began, I came back to my home. I heard at the Guildhall that the Corporation had offered the School to the Government for use as a hospital and my prospects of beginning the next term as Headmaster seemed doubtful. Nevertheless, I moved into the Headmaster's House early in September and term began after all."

Mr Parkinson – Centenary Booklet

Pupils' memories of the Great War

The First World War had a profound effect on the everyday lives of the orphans at the School. It was the first major conflict in which the lives of ordinary civilians were deliberately targeted, and German Zeppelins dropped bombs over London. The peace and security of life at school was suddenly under threat and no-one was unaffected.

Leonard Voller (1913–1922)

The start of the Great War

"I lived with my mother and sister Kathleen in Frinton-on-Sea in north Essex. On this particular day mother had sent us across the fields to the newsagent to buy a newspaper. I vividly recall, as we walked back, seeing the two words in large black letters across the front page – WAR DECLARED. I had just turned eight and Kathleen had not long had her sixth birthday.

Air raids

In September back at School, the London air raids started. Whenever German aircraft approached the area, maroon rockets were exploded overhead as a warning. Some daytime raids did take place but I cannot remember any over South London. If the rockets went off at night we had to get out of bed, put our shorts and jackets over our nightshirts and pick up our stockings (socks) from the flat clothes basket. This was where we kept our neatly folded clothes, which had to be arranged in the order in which they were taken off.

The gas-lights were put out, for the huge windows had no blackout curtains and no light must be seen from the outside. We then proceeded to the washroom, picking up our overcoats from the long cupboard as we passed, and waited in line for the last boys to catch up. A prefect or monitor would take us down to the long corridor at the bottom of the stairs, with those in the other two dormitories following us. A roll was called to check we were all down, after which we sat on the floor with our backs against the wall, while Masters sat on chairs spaced between our feet.

We were allowed to talk and encouraged to sing. Sometimes we would hear the ack-ack guns firing and occasionally the bursting of bombs. At last we would hear the Scout's bugle sounding the 'all clear' and we were permitted to go back to bed. We would be allowed an extra half-hour in bed next morning if we'd been kept up two hours or more.

In the morning we would scour every corner of the school grounds for pieces of shrapnel from the shells. If, on a rare occasion, a nosepiece was found, it had to be put in the school museum – a glass fronted cupboard.

I never saw a Zeppelin, but a few boys, whose homes were in London did so during the holidays. About five thousand were either killed or wounded from the air raids, and coastal bombardments.

Food rations

When I was in the Third Form we all used the last half hour of Friday afternoon lessons to cut the little squares from piles of ration books belonging to pupils, staff and any other employees who had their meals at the School. There must have been heavy food restrictions because of the rationing, but I can only remember one occasion when we refused to eat the meal put before us. It was breakfast time and the porridge was brown and tasted foul. We all put our spoons down and started to complain in unison. One of the monitors picked up his dish and took it to the Masters' table where it was duly smelt , tasted and immediately condemned. All the porridge was taken away and we were given two slabs of bread instead and a dollop of jam.

Women teachers

Two of our Masters were physically unfit for military service and stayed, but the places of those called up were taken over by Mistresses. Their arrival was greeted with consternation, but they were good teachers, so we soon started to respect them – except one we called 'Mum Greasy'. She had no idea how to handle a collection of boys and succeeded in offending us all. She would bring an oak drill stick from the gym to every class to use as a weapon – it was about three feet long and an inch thick. She would often clout us with it in her efforts to maintain discipline.

One evening, when middle school were going to bed, we all banged our feet up and down in unison, which was strictly forbidden in case the floor joints got damaged. As we stamped, on each step we chanted 'Mum Greasy'. She must have been furious, for she couldn't come up to our dormitory but just stood there at the bottom of the stairs.

Next morning we were paraded before the Head, who was very angry and gave us all a half-day detention. That meant two hours of boredom on a half-holiday. However, whether our action had anything to do with it or not, Mum Greasy did not return at the start of the new term.

Defence of the realm

There were no Home Guards in the Great War, but all men unfit for military service and able to stand, could enrol into a similar organisation. They had no uniform but wore a scarlet brassard on the right arm. The local squad used our grounds for drilling on Sunday mornings while we were at Church. If we returned before they had finished we had great entertainment watching their manoeuvres. The scarlet brassard bore two letters in black, "GR" for Georgius Rex, but we called them Gorgeous Wrecks.

The Silvertown disaster

One evening at School in 1917, I was reading a book while I leant against the wall near a window. The other chaps were spending their time as they did most evenings, playing chess, attending to their stamp collections, doing fretwork or just reading and talking. Suddenly an explosive blast shook the wall and rattled the windows. Immediately the gaslights were extinguished and our air raid drill was put into action. We sat in the corridor for quite a long while, wondering why no rockets had been fired, and there was not any sound of guns or bombs.

The Senior Master went to the School telephone box in the entrance hall and returned to tell us there had not been an air raid, but an explosion in east London. Next day we learnt a munitions factory over there had blown up and about sixty people had been killed. That was the great Silvertown disaster, and it had shaken our school six miles away.

The winter of 1917

The winter of 1917 was very cold with lots of snow. One morning a number of boys made a ring round me and snowballed me calling out 'German! German!'
A Master saw what was happening and stopped the bullying. That evening I sat in a corner pretending to read whilst I hid my face with my arm. Actually I was blubbing. I wrote a letter to my Mother asking her to take me away from the school.

Our letters had to be handed in unsealed and a proportion of them were censored. The next evening a monitor came into my room and told me to go to the Masters' Room. Two of the Masters wanted to know why I was asking to be taken away. One of them was the one who stopped the snowballing. They explained my name was like a German word but it did not mean I was German. They comforted me and told me it would never happen again. I was then asked if the letter could be put on the fire, as it would only cause my mother a lot of worry. I agreed and was never called 'German' again.

The summer of 1918

In the summer of 1918 some of the bigger boys were chosen to go down to a camp in Devon to pull flax for the war effort. I was too young. We learnt next term that the work was very hard, and although they were paid no-one wanted to do it again.

The end of the war

On the morning of 11th November 1918, there was a lot of suppressed excitement due to rumours the war might end that day. Later, while were sitting in class, one chap called out, 'look, Sir!' We all turned and looked out of the window as a balloon sailed past towing an enormous banner bearing one word – PEACE.

Classes were stopped amid loud cheering and a holiday was declared for two days."

Arthur Cole (left 1921)

"When the Zeppelins came over at night, we had to get up, take our blankets and go down and get in the corridor between the classrooms, where we sang all the old time war songs like 'Tipperary' to drown the sound of the guns. The older lads each had to look after one younger boy and make sure they weren't still asleep in bed!

One day when the Zeppelins came over in daylight we were all at Lambeth Swimming Baths, where we went weekly. No sooner were we in the water than we were told to get out and dress quickly as the King was coming to see us. Alas, no King but we were herded down into some cellars.

Anyway there was no damage to the School. I also recall during the war there were no book prizes. Instead winners were awarded War Savings Certificates."

Chas Chalmers (1920)

Summer camp experience

"In the first World War, aeroplane wings were covered in fabric made from flax. Since flax is made from roots of the plant, it followed that the plants had to be pulled and not cut. Flax was in very short supply, so the cadet contingent of the Freemen's School had to travel by train to Bridport. Lorries took us to our billets, which were disused, dilapidated, covered tennis courts. The building was ample inside but leaked in a large number of places so numerous buckets were placed around – woe betide anybody venturing to the outside latrines, especially in the dark!

The lorries collected us at 8.30am, dropping us off at various farms. The procedure was the first man pulled a swathe about a yard wide, placing the flax behind him for the binders to follow. Nobody could ease up or the formation would fail. Inside a week our hands were covered with thorns and horribly stung by nettles. Added to which our cadet kit was proving most unsuitable for farm work, so we used to take off our tunics.

One day a generous farmer gave us a jar of cider with predictable results - then working in the sun without a tunic gave me sunstroke. The billet was not an ideal sick bay. In due course I obtained permission to leave before the project finished. The farmer kindly gave me some apples and a rabbit, which was very welcome as food was in short supply. However, I rued the weight of the apples at the bottom of my kit bag, because when I got to London there was a strike on and I had to walk from Paddington Station to the Edgware Road, to try and get transport to my home in Cricklewood. I had to abandon the rabbit. I was 15 years old at the time and maybe this episode is the reason I've never been interested in camping."

Mary Emdin, (1918 to 1925) former Head Girl

Armistice

"One morning, during a Maths lesson with 'Daddy' Lowe, the Porter began to ring his hand-bell continuously. It was eleven o'clock on the 11th of November 1918. The Armistice had been signed. We were told that the war to end wars was over and not only were we to have a holiday but also all rules were cancelled for the day. Leaving everyone, I rushed down to the gym, let down the rope ladders and made it swing right across the whole floor. It felt great. Miss Ross discovered me and I had to stop, but I wasn't punished."

The Headmaster

Mr Parkinson managed to make a number of positive changes at the school during the Great War, despite the restrictions the conflict forced upon him. He wrote the following brief account of the changes achieved at the school during this time.

"I was told by the Chairman of the School Committee that I was to think out a scheme for the amalgamation of the two separate departments of boys and girls and to plan generally to bring the School up to date. He also warned me that I should come up against a certain amount of opposition to any reforms that I might suggest. The School at that time was confined to the orphan children of Freemen of the City of London. They were all boarders and left school on their fifteenth birthday. Their academic goal was the Cambridge Junior Examination.

During the years 1914-1918, with Zeppelin raids in the neighbourhood and the general disturbance of war, plus the fact that I was left with only one Assistant Master, it was difficult to make much progress. However the amalgamation of the boys' and girls' schools took place. The leaving age was raised to 16, and the curriculum was reformed.

At the end of the war the School was inspected by the Board of Education, who made suggestions for further reform, including the removal of the School from Brixton and the entry of fee-paying pupils, who were not orphans."

Casualties of the Great War

The number of casualties in the First World War was incredibly high. Despite the small number of pupils at the City of London Freemen's Orphan school, several 'old' boys lost their lives in the conflict. The following list is of staff and pupils killed in the Great War, taken from the memorial plaque in the Main House at Ashtead.

Howard Brooks	Augustus B Caesar
Albert E Clark	Valentine P G Day
Frederick D Goslin	Norman Kelly
William A Kerl	Oscar B Langford
Harold Machell	George H V May
Lester C. Morton	Walter G Price
Edward S. Wood	

A School Party visits the War Graves in 2001

Laura Holland was in the School party visiting the war graves at Ypres in 2001. This is an extract from her account. The experience really brought home to her the tragic loss of life during the Great War, seeing graves of boys younger than some in her own school year.

"We travelled to the Menin Gate where thousands upon thousands of names are engraved on the stone walls. I thought these were the names of all the lives lost in the Great War, but to my dismay I learned it was just the names of soldiers with no graves, soldiers who had left their homes and families and never returned.

While we were there, I was honoured to be chosen to lay the wreath for the thirteen Old Freemen who lost their lives, and especially for William Kerl whose name is inscribed on that wall. It was a very powerful moment, which I shall never forget. I felt it was a small demonstration of respect to make for the people who fought and suffered for people like me."

Before the group left for Ypres they had researched William Kerl and the Commonwealth War Grave Commission had sent them the information below – they were also given the exact position of his name on the memorial, which commemorates more than 54,000 officers and men who died at Ypres and have no grave.

WILLIAM AUSTEN KERL

Rifleman 1910

1st/16th Bn., London Regt (Queen's Westminster Rifles)

who died on

Friday 4th June 1915 aged 21

Son of Emily Kerl (nee Austen), of 63, Lewisham High Rd., London, and the late William James Kerl. Enlisted Aug. 1914. Educated at Freemen's School; apprenticed to Messrs John Howell & Co Ltd., Wholesale Drapers, of London.

chapter 8

TEACHING IN THE SCHOOL AFTER THE GREAT WAR

The First Inspection

When the Board of Education inspected the School in 1919, much of their criticism echoed the views of the Committee, in fact, reflected what the Committee had felt since the turn of the century. The premises at Brixton were no longer suitable, and the orphans should be segregated no longer. They needed to mix with children from normal homes.

The options were either to close the School completely, or move to new premises and make essential changes. These changes would involve accepting fee-paying pupils for the first time, and attracting better qualified staff by raising salaries.

The Board considered these possibilities carefully, and the financial consequences of closing the School, but fortunately decided it was more beneficial to move premises and introduce the recommended changes.

The Freemen's School Committee agreed with their decision and started looking for suitable properties within a 25 mile radius of London. They finally settled on the 88 acre Ashtead estate, and moved from Brixton in March 1926.

The following recollections from Old Boys and Girls are all about the staff at the School during the last decade at Brixton. As all the pupils at Brixton were orphans, the staff were enormously important to their development and happiness.

Mr Parkinson

Mary Emdin (1925) described the Headmaster as very tall and slim with a small toothbrush moustache, through which he hummed from time to time. He always wore his gown in class, taught Latin and Scripture and was an excellent teacher.

Known fondly as 'Parky' or 'Plank' by the pupils, the beginning and the end of his time as Headmaster were marked by world wars. He touched the lives of all his pupils, and many recall him with affection. Here is a short insight from **Len Voller (1913–1922)**.

"Mr Parkinson, or 'Parky' as we referred to him, was fair and firm and had a keen sense of humour. I experienced this one Sunday on the way to church. We were all lined up ready to march when the Masters arrived. Parky came out of his house and walked over. Towering above us (he was over six feet tall), he surveyed the ranks until our eyes met.

"Voller, I award you the O.B.E. What is the O.B.E?"

Relieved that I knew, I replied "The Order of the British Empire, Sir."

"Not in your case, laddie. You are going to be the Organ Blower at Epiphany."

As this award has never been officially gazetted, sadly I've been unable to use it."

Parkinson retained his sense of humour during all his years at the School. He related the following story about school life during the Second World War to former pupil John Pettman. "It was a summer's afternoon, the windows were open, and from my place in front of a quietly working class I noticed a savoury smell. Mmm! Something nice for lunch. Then I realised it was 3 pm. A tour up and down the aisles found the 'chef' frying half a sausage on a tiny methylated spirits cooker in his desk".

It says a lot for 'Plank' Parkinson that he thought this was amusing – though of course we don't know what he said to the 'chef' at the time.

The Old Freemen's Association, on 30th June 1996, dedicated a bench in the School grounds to the memory of their former Headmaster.

Arthur Lowe

Mary describes 'Daddy' Lowe as having thick grey curly hair and always wearing grey tweeds and a Norfolk jacket.

Chas Chalmers (1920) said:

"He was the heart of the School. Apart from being House Master, he taught maths and ran what sports we had. There was shinty on the tarmac, football also on the same hard surface, unless it was a match, in which case we used the Green in the Almshouses. He also introduced us to gardening and to this day I grow candytuft in his memory."

'Bob' Roberts

Mary remembers 'Bob' Roberts as "a strong bald headed man, who always dressed in tweeds and gave interesting and easy to follow lessons." He was the Art Master and also took poetry in the higher forms.

Mr Brown

Described by 'Chas' Chalmers as 'a very dedicated man who taught carpentry,' he also encouraged the children to enjoy gardening.

Ronald Everest (1918-1928) recalls:

"During the very cold winter months I, with other boys, used to wait for Mr Brown, the Carpentry Master, to open up his Carpenter's Shop. Then we woud collect up all the pieces of waste wood and shavings left from the previous day's lessons, and light up his circular cast-iron boiler. It was very comforting during those very cold mornings.

Sometimes I helped him with his allotment. During my adult life I have worked several allotments and still today grow potatoes in my garden. Although we had all lost our fathers, there were the opportunities to learn or be taught many of the everyday things at the School with teachers like Mr Brown, which others more fortunate learnt at home."

Len Voller (1913-1922) remembers:

"Mr Brown, known by us as Old Brownie, was our Carpentry Master and it was a pleasure to work to his instructions. Old Brownie hated boys whistling. One day he hit me hard with a piece of wood on the back of my head, and bellowed at me to stop whistling. When I picked it up, I found it was a block of mahogany from which I made a dove-tail marker. I've kept it and used it ever since. In our last term he let us make anything we liked to take home with us. I made a crockery cupboard, with a cutlery drawer, for my mother."

Miss Cameron

The Matron was a formidable Scottish woman with a dog called Rory. When not on duty she could often be seen with a golf club, hitting a ball for Rory to fetch. Her strong accent made her very difficult to understand and many mistakes were made because of it. Mary says: "She behaved as though she was an exalted person and we, unable to obey her simplest commands, were all fools. If she were cross with Rory, he would rush out and try to attack us, but we just shied away laughing."

Ron Everest remembers: 'One event we looked forward to was Matron's party for her dog, Rory. Each year she would invite the youngest boys and girls to a party to celebrate the dog's birthday. She provided a special tea and we played games afterwards.'

Miss Robins

Miss Robins was a Kipling fan who had a life-long love of India and all things Indian. As she grew older, it seems she became increasingly strict. She died unexpectedly after a short illness in 1922.

Miss Hutton (taught from 1903–1936)

Headmistress for many years, first at Brixton, then Ashstead, Miss Hutton was a very popular and much loved teacher.

Daisy Wiard (1928-32) says:

"To many seven-year-old youngsters entering boarding school, meeting the Headmistress was a daunting experience. However, Miss Hutton's warm friendly greeting and introduction into our new 'family' soon dispelled our fears and helped us to settle down happily. Her stern discipline was tempered with fairness and kindness. As a teacher she was also an understanding caring confidante ever ready and willing to listen to problems and dispense advice and guidance.

Her enthusiasm for teaching, whether English, Singing or Drama, or imparting a great understanding of the works of William Shakespeare, was inspiring and gave a great insight to her talent as a sole producer and director who brought out the best in all her performers.

Miss Hutton was a shining example and guide to us. She helped us overcome our sorrows and happily shared our joys. We remember her with great affection and appreciate the lasting influence she had on our lives."

A garden to her memory, together with a commemorative plaque, was planted by the Old Freemen's Association on 28th June 1998. It is situated in front of the Clubhouse.

Miss Sparks

Mary Emdin recalls that Miss Sparks, who taught domestic science, was very small and very efficient. In the Middle School the boys learnt Wood and Metal-work whilst the girls took Cookery, Dressmaking, Needlework and Laundry. Mary admits to finding the needlework rather boring as it always consisted of making calico nightdresses for deprived babies. Miss Sparks would sometimes stand on a stool or a chair to make herself more imposing and could be bitingly sarcastic to those who annoyed her. She later married 'Daddy' Lowe.

Miss Young

According to Mary, Miss Sparks' successor was tall, fair and very good looking, vivacious and smiling. "Needlework suddenly turned from drudgery to art. Gone were the calico nightdresses for the poor. Instead we had coloured material and silks to embroider our work, which we were allowed to take home. Handkerchief sachets, nightdress cases and even Dressmaking were now encouraged."

chapter 9

LIFE AT SCHOOL UNTIL THE MOVE TO ASHTEAD

As outlined in the previous chapter, following the Great War, the Committee continued to seek suitable new premises for the School in order to expand the curriculum, end the segregation of orphans from other children, and benefit from some green space. Meanwhile, life went on as usual at the City of London Freemen's Orphan School.

The following recollections of pupils there at the time allow us a view of how the School was run during the decade before the move to Ashtead in 1926.

Ronald Everest (1918-1928)

The Death of My Grandfather

"I was a double orphan before I entered the Brixton School at a very young age. I was still only nine when one day in the middle of term the staff were informed of the death of my grandfather. When they told me I was naturally very upset and I remember the French Master taking me to the Tuck Shop where he bought me several bags of sweets to cheer me up.

Pocket Money and the Tuck Shop

The tuck shop was very important to all the pupils. At the beginning of each school term we gave our pocket money to the Master in charge of it, then on Saturday mornings we were allowed small amounts of money from the 'bank', for sweets and other items we wanted.

The Conduct Mark System

Each week our names were entered on what was called the Conduct Sheet. Then Masters and Prefects could deduct marks according to the severity of our wrong-doing or low standard of work. We were allocated various punishment duties for loss of marks, such as cleaning boots, bed making and clearing tables after meals. But if at the end of the week your total was over 20 marks lost, you had to report to Mr. Parkinson's study on Monday morning for six strokes of the cane.

Handwriting

This was considered so important it warranted a lesson each week and a prize on prize day for the pupil with the best handwriting. We had special writing exercise books with perfect script samples and spaces underneath to copy them three times. Then we learnt how to join up our script writing to write programmes for plays. We were not allowed to print in capitals.

Sports Day 1920 – R.E. Everest

School Flag – School Archives

Games

We played football and cricket matches on the grassed area in front of the Freemen's Almshouses, next to the boys' playground. The girls used their own grassed playground area. During the summer term, a special day was allocated as Sports Day and the grassed area in the Almshouses was marked out as a sports arena. Competition was between either the School Houses or individuals.

Sunday Activities

No games or sports of any description were allowed, as indeed was the custom in most Victorian homes. We dressed in our best suits after breakfast and walked along Ferndale Road, in a crocodile, to the Emmanuel Church in Clapham, for our own church service. Certain pupils were chosen for the choir, and they borrowed the local choir's cassocks.

After lunch we again walked in crocodile file to Brockwell Park or other parts of the Brixton neighbourhood. After tea, we attended a prayer service in the Dining Hall.

Being a Sub Monitor

I believe I was the youngest sub-monitor. At the age of 12, I had to look after the very young boys and supervise their prep period, sitting in the Master's chair on the raised platform. When they finished, I gave them their supper – a mug of milk and biscuits – then took them in line upstairs to the dormitory. I made sure they washed and cleaned their teeth before putting them to bed. Afterwards I would finish my own prep before the senior boys came up to bed. During the day I was responsible for supervising their meals. I sat at the head of the dining table and cut up the long loaves of bread for them – I also had to keep them quiet and correct their table manners. Later it was my job to supervise clearing the meal tables, bed making or boot cleaning.

My First Geometry Set

In the third form I was given a box of instruments comprising a ruler, a pair of compasses, some set squares, several pencils and a rubber. I loved them. Using them to produce neat and accurate drawing is a skill I have used all my adult life – I even designed the School flag."

Len Voller (1913-1922)

Prize Day

"Prize Day each July was like Christmas Day to us. Tiered seating was erected on the platform at the west end of the hall. The boys and girls sat on the tiered seating with the smallest pupils on the top tier. At the bottom sat the Lord Mayor and the Sheriff, the Committee and the Headmaster, along with lots of aspidistras. Parents and other guests sat in the main part of the hall facing us.

Hall on Prize Day – School Archives

Prize Day was the only day of the year that we had blancmange and jellies, with cake for tea. The only other time cake was available was on a pupil's birthday when a cake was sent from home. After inspection of the parcel to remove letters and presents, the cake would be taken away to re-appear at the tea table in front of the birthday boy. He would cut the cake into a certain number of slices and then, list in one hand and cake in the other, he would offer a slice to his friends on the list. Thus were friendships cemented and foes made, the foes being those who expected a piece but did not get one.

Swimming

In the summer months the boys in the upper classes would line up on a Thursday morning to receive swimming trunks rolled up in a towel. We would then walk two-by-two from Brixton to Lambeth Baths and back. When a boy could show that he was able to swim a width of the bath, he was allowed to swim to the deep end.

Brothers and Sisters

On Sunday afternoon after lunch there was a period called 'Brothers and Sisters'. During this half hour my sister Kathleen and I met in the hall and sat on opposite sides of the table, exchanging letters from home, news and little gifts. We had no other contact with each other except when relations came to visit.

Healthcare

At School, minor and imagined ailments were all cured by three medicines; cod liver oil for the not-so-robust, a peppermint flavoured liquid called 'whitewash' for stomach ailments, and for coughs, colds and sore throats, the back of the throat was brushed with iodine.

A doctor used to visit the School for the annual health inspection and thereafter when necessary. The nurse used to carry out 'head scratching' once a month with a fine toothed comb. A couple of barbers would cut our hair after the head scratching."

Daisy Wiard (1928)

Daisy was one of a family of four, all educated at the School.

Starting at the School

"For a seven year old, entry into an orphanage was a terrifying ordeal, but I quickly overcame the terror when I was placed into the care of a Senior. She was responsible for my well-being and neat appearance. Very comforting for me, but probably a real nuisance for her.

Uniform

A uniform was issued to me, all marked with an identification number. I had a dark, box pleated dress with detachable square white collar, white overall, two pairs of black shoes (one for indoors and one for outdoors), a dark winter coat and a stiff flat topped straw brimmed hat.

The hat was known as a 'barge' and did not fit properly. It spun round every time I turned my head, often leading to stifled giggles at inappropriate times, for which we were punished. The barge finally fitted when I got bigger.

We were punished for running, talking, loitering or slouching in corridors. We were expected to stand upright, with no round shoulders and to walk briskly at all times. If you did not manage it, you were made to walk up and down stairs balancing a book on your head, until you got the right posture.

Segregation

We were cut off from the outside world at the School, and apart from mixed classes, boys and girls were also strictly segregated. Our Sunday morning walk along Ferndale Road to the local church gave us a glimpse of an outside world we had no part of. Also on Sundays, brothers and sisters were allowed to meet in the Dining Hall for two hours. No other contact with them was allowed.

Visitors

Once a month we were allowed a visit from two relatives between 2pm and 4pm. They could only bring us fruit, no other food or sweets, and we had to hand it over immediately to a duty monitor, who labelled it and put it in a cupboard. The next morning a staff member would hand it out again.

The boys received their visitors in their own playground if the weather was good, or in their classrooms. Girls saw theirs in their classrooms or the gymnasium. Brothers and sisters could meet their relatives in the staff garden between the two playgrounds, or the Dining Hall if it was wet.

If our relatives gave us pocket money, we were allowed to spend it at the tuck shop on Saturdays. Juniors were allowed to spend one penny, Intermediates tuppence and Seniors threepence. All other sweets were banned. Although life was restrictive, it was enjoyable. We soon learned team spirit and how to mix well with the others.

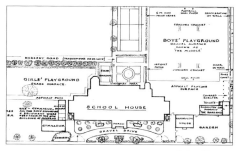

School Layout

Leisure time

Leisure hours were spent in our classrooms, or in the playground if the weather was good. A railway line ran along one side of the playground, so we would spend time counting passing trains, and waving at the passengers. Girls could use the gymnasium for dancing, singsongs, and games.

Sleeping arrangements

Girls had three dormitories, one senior and two junior. The senior one was above the girls' classrooms and the juniors were above the boys' classrooms. They were connected by a balcony spanning the width of the entrance hall. There was also a Mistress's bedroom next to each dormitory. The boys' dormitories were on the second floor. A prefect and monitor slept in each dormitory. We obeyed a strict rota for getting up each morning. A Mistress often made a surprise visit to check for anyone lying in, a punishable offence.

Meals

We went straight from our dormitories down into the Dining Hall for breakfast. Girls sat at one end and the boys, who came in through a separate door, at the other. Staff sat on the platform.

We enjoyed three good, adequate meals every day, but there were no second helpings and we had to eat every morsel of food provided. We would secretly pass uneaten food along to a sister or friend to eat, so we could avoid punishment.

We had a daily set menu throughout the whole term. Breakfast was porridge, bread and butter and a mug of coffee. The mugs were shaped like barrels so they rolled down the table if they got knocked over. We were allowed 20 minutes to eat breakfast.

A two course dinner was served at 1.00pm. The first course was roast beef or lamb and boiled potatoes in their skins. We only had greens on Thursdays, and sometimes a bowl of soup replaced the meat. The second course was always a delicious pudding.

We had tea at 5.00pm. It was bread and jam with a mug of tea. We only had butter on Wednesdays, when there was no jam. On Sundays we enjoyed a cake and butter, but again no jam.

Finally, after prep, we had a mug of hot milk with a large hard biscuit known as a 'chud', specially made for the School by Huntley and Palmers. Although the diet was very plain, it was enough to keep us all healthy. The sick bay was rarely in great demand.

Table manners

Only quiet conversation was allowed at meal times, then a loud bell and the rest of the meal was eaten in total silence and contemplation. It was considered unladylike to 'bite' bread. It was supposed to be cut into small pieces and popped into the mouth cleanly. The female staff consisted of four Mistresses. They were strict about enforcing school rules, but were nevertheless very caring and tried to make our lives enjoyable."

Mary Emdin, 1918 to 1925 (former Head Girl)

"Mother took me to School with a health certificate from the home doctor. I had to present this to the school doctor, after I had changed into my uniform. All our clothes opened down the front, which allowed the doctor easy access to test our lungs and heart. He measured our chest expansion while we took deep breaths, and compared the results at the start of each term. The School provided our uniform and I thought there were far too many garments.

But even with the generous supply of clothing, we were sometimes really cold on winter nights. We had to keep the fan-lights open, so all the heat from the lovely hot water pipes round the dormitory went straight outside. Sometimes we were tempted to wrap our flannel vests round our feet, but if we were caught we were given three bad points. Mostly we thought this too great a risk.

Miss Hutton & Girls – Centenary Booklet

Dormitories

There were three dormitories: 'the Fifteen' for the tiniest, 'the Ten' for older newcomers and 'the Big Dormitory' for everyone else. To get to the Ten and the Fifteen you had to walk through the Big and across the balcony over the entrance hall. It all seemed vast and lonely as I went over on my first night.

We were shown our beds and had to fold the counterpane, and arrange it over the bar at the foot of the bed. After kneeling by the bed for private prayers, we were told to undress and carefully fold all our clothes (except our outer uniform) and put them into a basket under the bed. Our outer garments were draped over the chair next to our beds.

After washing and cleaning our teeth, we brushed our hair. Then we had to show the brush to the prefect to check that all hairs had been combed out of it.

We were not allowed to speak after lights out, but we quickly learnt the deaf and dumb alphabet from other children, using it whenever silence was the rule. Every night we would lie on our stomachs, pushing our hands through the bars of the bed where they could be seen by the shaft of light from the bathroom, and communicate with each other for quite a while.

Rules and punishments

Lists of the School rules and penalties were kept under our desk lids. Punishments were fair but exacting. One punishment was 'wearing the white overall' which involved wearing a white tabard, in silence, for two days. We also lost holiday time through accumulated bad points. The first Monday of every month was a holiday, when you could do what you liked all day (within the school rules of course). I lost the whole day's holiday in my first month.

I remember getting bad marks for running in the corridor, talking in line, keeping things in my desk other than schoolwork, not having my hair in two plaits, and for not eating my fat at dinner time.

The death of Miss Robins

Although Miss Robins was not a favourite teacher of mine, I was sad to hear of her death when we returned from our Christmas holiday in 1922. Miss Hutton, her successor, sent for me in her study and said: "Miss Robins spoke of you, Mary. She died in great pain, yet she thought about you. She told me that however unlikely it may seem, you will do well and become Head Girl before you leave." From this day forwards I stopped getting into trouble.

Becoming a School 'mother'

Some months later I was considered fit to be a school 'mother', which meant I was put in charge of a new girl. Bunny Davis, from Canada, was a little, round faced, jolly child who smiled a lot. She was a big responsibility. Your 'daughter' had to be tidy, punctual and keep out of trouble. You could lose points if she did not.

On Saturday mornings we had a mending session. As well as seeing to your own clothes, you had to teach your 'daughter' how to mend hers. When there was not any mending, we strengthened the toes and heels of our stockings with ornamental darning. The good thing about it was we were allowed to talk. Unfortunately mending was always followed by the weekly visit from the Headmistress, going over the week's lost points and looking for reasons why you had transgressed!

Sports Day

That same year, I won the prize for High Jump. It was a fluke. They had reached the height where all the other entrants had knocked down the rope and I was the last to try. Just as I jumped, a starting pistol went off for the boys' hurdles and I raised my legs a little higher in panic. I cleared the rope and won the prize, a very nice attaché case.

We had a sporting event peculiar to the School called Pilarius Lucio – the balls of light. Entrants had to juggle three balls, without pause, indefinitely. The one who carried on longest won. Girls who were experts went on for nearly half the afternoon.

Committee night

On a Friday night, once a term, the smell of rich food and cigars pervaded our corridor. It was the Committee night, when the Sheriffs and Aldermen from the City of London came for a meal and to discuss a Report on the progress of the School.

We were kept well away from it all, but the Sheriff of the Year was always very affable and sure to give us all some little treat, such as an outing, or an apple and orange each. One even arranged for a Concert Party to come and entertain us. Unfortunately he did not check what kind of show it was, and it turned out to be a musical sprinkled with risqué words. We did not get any more Concert Parties after that.

My first boyfriend

At School one term I decided I must have a boyfriend. At meals I would spend my time squinting down at the boys' end of the dining hall, looking for a boy I fancied. Leonard Voller seemed very nice, and conveniently he was my friend Kathleen's brother. He had golden hair, a turned up nose and an innocent air. I caught his eye and he smiled.

I told Kathleen I liked her brother and she told him on 'Brothers' Sunday' when they met for an hour in the hall. Then she reported back. He was pleased I liked him. After that our contact was through passed messages, waves and smiles.

One day in French class, Leonard asked the Master if he could lend me his dictionary.

Inside I found a poem he had composed about me and I was delighted. I now had a regular boy friend. Leonard was a year older, at fourteen, and about two inches taller than me. We had little chance of ever being alone together so we devised a scheme to meet at the School nurse's dispensary. We both reported stomach pains on the same morning, after breakfast, and were sent upstairs to Nurse's quarters. There we chatted rather shyly, drinking the hated gritty, white mixture we called 'whitewash'. The peppermint flavour repeated all day.

The School Play

Although we did not belong to the Dramatic Society, we volunteered to be members of the crowd in Julius Caesar, so we were in the Christmas performance. The School play was always performed on two evenings. The choice of play depended on what was set for the Senior Cambridge exam that year.

On the first night the pupils, staff and everyone working for the School, inside or out, were invited. It was a kind of dress rehearsal. On the second night the City of London Committee members and their friends came, together with parents of pupils in the play.

Upper School volunteers painted the scenery, while the curtains and footlights were the responsibility of the boys' science group. The costumes came from Manchester, in big square basket trunks, and everyone got really excited when they were opened.

After the show on the second night, we had a performers' supper. Boys were allowed to invite girls to eat with them, so naturally Leonard asked me. We had sausage and mash, followed by jelly and custard, which was a traditional stage supper. We felt very grown up and special. This was the end of my time in Middle School. The following term I entered the Upper School, which meant I could have my hair in one plait instead of two, and gained new privileges.

Life in the Upper School

I went first to my new classroom, which was for fifth and sixth formers. It was lighter and more modern, with single desks, which had seats with comfortable round, adjustable backs. Fifth formers sat near the door and sixth formers nearer the window. At the back of the room was a coal fire with a fireguard topped with a brass rail, about seat height. However, anyone sitting on it lost a mark immediately and unfortunately it clanked loudly when you stood up.

Above the fire-place was the Upper School motto: 'Self control and self denial are the two chief health giving virtues'. The Middle School motto was: 'You can if you think you can' while the Lower School had: 'Think and Thank'.

The Power of the Mind

Now we were in Upper School, Miss Hutton came to talk to us on Sunday afternoons. She was a great believer in the power of the mind, and gave us mental exercises in holding an image as long as we could. We sat with our eyes closed, concentrating hard, then raised a hand when the image (often a rose) faded. She told us part of our minds controlled breathing, circulation, digestion and minor wound healing. If we believed and concentrated on the idea, we would alert our immune system and keep well.

Almost 70 years after they left School, Mary and her friend Kathleen Cody (née Voller) came to an Old Freemen's Day to look round the School. The School has four of the certificates that Kathleen earned for Needlework awarded by the London Institute of Needlework between 1922-1925."

Mary Emdin and Kathleen Cody née Voller in 1992 – Pat Scholes

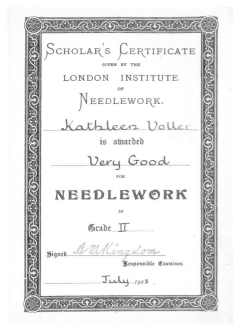

Needlework Certificate – Cody Family

Ronald Everest (1918-1928)

A Visit to Ashtead Park

"During the last term at Brixton, the School staff and pupils were taken on open-top buses for their first visit to Ashtead Park. This was a very exciting day out in the country and a welcome change from routine.

We passed several conifer trees lining the roads up to the Park and broke off small branches. The smell was so wonderful, I'll never forget it. We had tremendous fun roaming the gardens. I especially remember the large room at the end of the House, now the music rooms, which was a hot house full of tropical plants. I was also very impressed by the stable block with its large clock.

Stable Block – School Archives

Before the end of our last term at Brixton, we were all presented with a photograph of the new School building, from the Chairman of the Governors. I had mine framed and it still hangs in my home."

chapter 10

A SHORT HISTORY OF ASHTEAD PARK

Ashtead Park has a history long pre-dating the elegant eighteenth century house seen by the pupils on their first visit. Archaeological research has found evidence of Celtic, Roman and Saxon occupation of the site. There is also a legend that the Wych elm that stood near the lower drive was a Witan meeting place in the Tenth Century, Witan being the Anglo-Saxon word for Council or Parliament. The park, or 'stede' is described in the Domesday Book, as having boundaries very similar to the present parish ones.

In Tudor times, a Manor house existed next to the churchyard, and some of its foundations were discovered during the construction of the Old Freemen's Memorial Clubhouse.

Sir Robert Howard bought the estate in 1680, and used it as his main residence. As Chancellor of the Exchequer he felt he needed a more imposing home, in keeping with his position. He built an elegant house on the site of the present building, and used the Tudor building as a dairy. He stocked the Park with deer and added a lake and an avenue of trees. The estate was used to entertain royalty – in their time Charles II, James II and William III all visited the house. Apparently the King William Gate (on to Farm Lane) was put in just so the King could get to the racecourse more easily – and the lime walk, running from the House to the church, was also planted as a tribute to him.

King William Gate – School Archives

Tudor Farmhouse
Reproduced by permission of Surrey Library Service

Lady Fielding inherits

Sir Robert's daughter in law, Lady Diana Fielding, inherited the estate, and was a great benefactress to the village. The almshouses she founded are still in use at the corner of Park Lane, and there is a tribute to her on the front door.

Lady Diana died childless and the estate reverted to the Howards, eventually coming to a female heir to the estate called Frances Howard. Her husband, Richard Bagot, changed his name to Howard after she inherited.

By now the house had been neglected for some time and was no longer habitable, so the couple built a new one. While it was being built, the family moved into a house in the grounds known then as the Gardener's House – later the Headmaster's House.

Picture of the house without wings – School Menu

The new house was designed by the Italian Joseph Bonomi, and built by Sir Thomas Wyatt. It was a square brick house, faced with white stone. The basement of the former house was kept, and is still used by the Music and P.E. Departments.

In 1880 the entire estate was sold to Sir Thomas Lucas, a wealthy industrial tycoon who lavished vast sums on improving the Park. He obtained permission to build the Rookery Hill road through the estate and a stone bridge to cross the gully, together with lodges and gates. He enlarged the house to include a billiard room on one side and an exotic conservatory on the other, paved with white marble and heated by a special boiler house below. He then planted a shrubbery and a formal Italian garden, installed gravelled terraces and built an ornamental balustrade around the whole mansion.

Picture of the house with wings – O.F.A. Archives

When he died, the house was purchased for a Greek banker, Pantia Ralli, as a wedding present from his mother. Ralli installed electric lighting all along the drives, and a lift in the house when he could no longer get up the stairs easily. The proud owner of a fleet of cars, rumour has it he built Teddy Bear Cottage for his chauffeur.

Ashtead welcomed him because he employed a large number of local people and was keen to be involved in the village life. The Annual Fair and the Flower Show were held in the grounds. When he died in1924, his widow decided to sell the estate. And so it was possible for the Corporation of London to purchase the House and grounds for the School in 1925.

Teddy Bear Cottage – W. Davies CLOGA

chapter 11

THE BIG MOVE

Christmas 1925

The Christmas term of 1925 was probably an unsettling time for the children, as they were all keenly aware of the impending move away from London. It was a significant change, especially for those children who had only ever lived in the city. Aware of their anxieties, the Chairman of the Governors, Percy Vincent, sent each of them a Christmas card with a picture of their new home at Ashtead Park, which many of the children kept framed. It was also an opportunity for the remaining parents or guardians to see where the children were going to live.

Memories of the move

Miss Hutton, the Senior Mistress at Brixton, spent a great deal of time and energy telling the children all about the new school prior to the move. Daisy Wiard, a former pupil, recalls: "Her enthusiasm fired one and all with excitement, long before the final move. Her vivid descriptions of our new home and surrounding grounds seemed too beautiful to be believed." The pupils and staff started the unenviable task of labelling everything and packing it away carefully. A special trip was arranged for everyone to visit the new School. According to Daisy: "Thanks to Miss Hutton's superb description of every nook and cranny of the mansion and grounds, we soon felt the beauty and serenity rub off on us. We could not wait to move"

The first term at Ashtead

After the Easter holidays, all the pupils were incredibly keen to get back to school for their first term at Ashtead. They could not believe their luck when they arrived and discovered the School rules had been dropped, though this was just a temporary bonus. All their letters home were full of their amazement at the park and the surrounding beauty, and according to Daisy, a lot of their enthusiasm was inspired by Miss Hutton.

Apparently she spent many happy hours sitting in her Dutch garden, deep in contemplation or reading. Pupils loved it if she asked them to help her weed it, as she infused everyone with the joy and appreciation she herself felt being in the countryside.

Christmas Card & Envelope – O.F.A. Archives

Dutch Gardens – O.F.A. Archives

The Official photo of School assembled outside Octagonal Room – School Archives

The official opening

Although all seventy pupils had moved from Brixton to Ashtead Park during the Easter holidays, the official opening by the Lord Mayor, Sir William Pryke, did not take place until June 17th 1926. This photo was taken on the big day.

Front – Miss Cameron (Matron and Housekeeper); Mr Parkinson (Headmaster, also taught History and Geography); Miss Hutton (Senior Mistress, also taught English Literature and Music).

Behind – Mr Roberts (Art, Religious Instruction and Sport); Mr Dennis (French and General Subjects – left1926); Mr Lowe (Mathematics and Science); Miss Bradley (Religious Instruction and General Subjects), Miss Hall (Needlework and General Studies) and Miss Gascoigne (Domestic Science).

The School changes its name

In July 1927, the name of the School changed and became the City of London Freemen's School. 'Orphan' was dropped from the title because the School had started admitting fee-paying boys as both boarders and day pupils. However, to this day, the School still accepts orphans of the Freemen of the City to be educated and if necessary boarded for no fee.

The Foundationers, as the original members of the School were known, regarded the new pupils with suspicion. Parkinson later recalled finding the first day-boy roped to a tree in the grounds. But as the School grew he observed, 'the Foundationers grew less in numbers each succeeding year and the fee-paying pupils applying for admission exceeded the number of vacant places.'

By 1927 the orphan pupils had been joined by twenty day pupils and five boarders. Of the 70 orphans, 14 were children of the City Imperial Volunteers, the regiment raised in the City for service in the Boer War.

Denise van Mentz (1926-1936)

Two new pupils, Brian and Denise van Mentz, arrived in 1926 from South Africa. Denise was born in Johannesburg in 1919 and her brother Brian was three years older. She recalls: "Father died suddenly when I was five, so mother travelled to England to arrange for our education and set things up for us to join the City of London Freemen's School. When we arrived at School I was completely unskilled. In South Africa I had had a nanny to dress me and we never wore shoes, so I had no idea how to tie up shoe laces.

1928/9 Rugby Team – O.F.A. Archives

One of my earliest English memories is the year of the coal strike when the School had to burn wood. My brother Brian showed the bigger boys how to chop and cut up wood for the furnaces. Then it snowed and I wondered what all the salt was. I could not understand why the snow melted when I brought it indoors.

We had to strip our beds each morning, then kneel on our basket of clothes to say our prayers before we made the beds again. The girls were on the second floor, which had larger rooms with high ceilings. The boys' dormitories were on the third floor, and used to be the servants' quarters when it was a private house. Miss Hutton, the Headmistress had her own suite on the girl's floor near the dormitories, with a cosy wood fire in it."

According to Charles Lawrence (left 1930), the photograph of the 1928-1929 rugby team includes a boy called Edwards, the first day boy and the first non-foundation scholar to play for the School.

Millennium Plaque – O.F.A. Archives

Preserving memories of Brixton

Very few reminders were kept of the old School at Brixton and the children were encouraged to make a fresh start. New pupils knew little of the history of the School apart from a few continued traditions, and occasional stories they heard from the seventy Foundationers. Old pupils could not even visit the old building as it was pulled down in 1927 to make way for police married quarters.

It is only recently that some of those who remember Brixton have been trying to record their memories for posterity. Ronald Everest (pupil 1918–1928) etched a plaque commemorating the years at Brixton, which he donated to the School. He attended the special unveiling ceremony on Old Freemen's Day in 2000.

chapter 12

THE START OF THE ASHTEADIAN AND THE HOUSE SYSTEM

The Ashteadian

The Ashteadian magazine was first produced in October 1928. Past pupils were invited to contribute to 'maintain the connection between former scholars and the School, to foster further personal friendships and to foster a spirit of loyalty.'

A popular item in the early magazines was the careers section. Each magazine featured a different occupation, and gave readers full details of the kind of opportunities available. There was also a past pupils' section, and interviews with any leaving staff. The rest of the magazine was filled with rugby fixtures and school gossip, with plenty of attention given to frozen pipes and book shortages.

For a long time, the Ashteadian came out twice a year. Simple booklets with plain covers, each was inscribed with the City crest and a volume number. In May 1966 this changed to a white cover with a purple band. Still keeping the City crest, the cover now featured a title 'The Journal of the City of London Freemen's School.' Illustrated covers were not introduced until October 1975, and even then the magazine retained its slim shape.

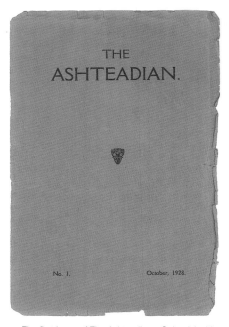

The first issue of The Ashteadian – School Archives

The House System

In 1928 the School also introduced the House system. The boys' houses were named after three famous former Lord Mayors - Gresham, Hale and Whittington.

The girls settled on Wren and Gayer. Here is a brief biography of each dignitary, giving an idea of why they were chosen.

Hale

Hale was an obvious choice, named after Warren Stormes Hale, the School's founder. Born in 1791, Hale was orphaned at an early age. A Tallow Chandler and Master of the Livery Company, he rose to be Sheriff 1858-60, and Lord Mayor 1884-5. A fervent educationalist, Hale died in 1872.

Sir Thomas Gresham

Born in 1519, by the age of thirty-five Sir Thomas Gresham was regarded by his contemporaries as something of a financial wizard. Henry VIII had sent him to look after English interests in Antwerp, the banking capital of Europe.

Although his methods were not entirely honest, he achieved remarkable results, paying off England's high debts to the Netherlands.

W.S. Hale – School Archives

Grasshopper Sign – O.F.A. Archives

Sir Thomas Gresham School Archives

A more permanent reminder of his career is the Royal Exchange, which he founded in 1565 as a meeting place for merchants and financiers. He also left money in his will to set up Gresham College, which became the main centre of scientific education for the next hundred years. Gresham was also a foundling, and adopted the grasshopper as his emblem. It can still be seen on some bank buildings today.

Richard Whittington

Richard Whittington, better known as Dick Whittington, is the Lord Mayor everyone remembers. Born around 1358, he died in 1423 after amassing great wealth as a Mercer. As an Alderman, Sheriff and Lord Mayor he was in a position to make loans to both Henry IV and Henry V, and his rise to fortune caught the imagination of all aspiring Londoners.

A generous benefactor, he founded a college, a hospital, a church and almshouses. He also left money to the Mercers' Company for distributing pensions and grants. Immortalised in pantomime, the first performance of Dick Whittington was at Covent Garden in 1814. Incidentally, his famous cat was more likely to have been a barge, the old French word for barge being 'achat.' There is a blue plaque commemorating Dick Whittington at 20, College Hill EC4.

Richard Whittington – Mercers Company

Girls' houses

Wren

Sir Christopher Wren was born in Wiltshire in 1632. Educated at Westminster School and Wadham College, Oxford, he graduated with a Masters degree in 1651. At 25 he became Chair of Astronomy at Gresham College, London. In 1663 Wren first tried his hand as an architect, designing Pembroke College Chapel, Cambridge. In 1666 Wren submitted a plan for the reconstruction of St. Paul's Cathedral which was accepted by King Charles II. Six days later the Great Fire of London destroyed the cathedral completely. Within days of this disaster Wren presented his plan for re-building the city. Broad, tree-lined avenues and classical architectural lines completely changed the warren of alleys and streets.

Wren's influence spread across the British Isles taking in Tom Tower at Christ's Church Oxford, Trinity College Library and and the Royal Hospital at Chelsea. He also re-modelled Kensington Palace, the Naval Hospital, Greenwich and Hampton Court Palace. To this day, Christopher Wren is seen as the most influential British architect.

Gayer

Sir John Gayer was Lord Mayor of London in 1647. He is mainly remembered for one of his adventures in the Arabian Desert. He became separated from his caravan and was completely lost when he encountered a lion. He prayed to God to save him, and the lion retreated. Believing his prayers to have been answered, he gave all the profits from the expedition to charity. Later he became a beneficiary to Christ's Hospital and rebuilt the church of St Katherine Cree.

chapter 13

THE YEARS LEADING UP TO THE SECOND WORLD WAR

A second inspection by the Board of Education came far sooner than the School would have liked. Staff and pupils had hardly settled in to their new surroundings at Ashtead when the inspectors arrived. Their report was not very favourable.

Generally the standard of work was deemed higher than before, but the inspectors felt that some areas of the curriculum still needed improving. They recommended the School employ more qualified staff to help them achieve this. However, their biggest criticism concerned the disproportionately low number of girl pupils.

The Committee had decided the School should accept fee-paying boys as soon as everyone was settled at Ashtead. But no girls had enrolled since the move, and between May 1926 and May 1929 their number dropped from 42 to 34. Finally, in 1933, it was decided to admit fee-paying girls. Unfortunately by then the School was perceived by the public as a boys' school, and it was many years before there was anything like equal numbers. In 1938, boys out numbered girls by 160 to 34.

Staff

Though there were fewer teachers in those days, there were also proportionally fewer pupils. This meant teachers knew all the students well, especially as all staff performed several tasks outside their own curriculum duties. Games for example, including coaching, was simply taken by the more athletic members of staff. Other teachers helped run out of school clubs and entertainments, including school trips. Overseas visits started in Easter 1933, when two of the teachers took twenty-four boys to Belgium.

Even the Headmaster had to take his share of extra duties. Former pupil Margaret Gillatt, who left in 1940, remembers Mr and Mrs Parkinson being in charge of the 1939 choir outing when they all went to play cricket on Leith Hill. The boys played the girls, and they did not use a proper cricket ball because it was too hard. Afterwards they all went for tea at a local hostelry in Friday Street, run by the mother of an ex pupil. The following photo was taken at the end of the day and apparently the girls were allowed to take off their panama hats (at the time a compulsory part of the girls' summer uniform) just for the picture.

Photo of Choir Outing July 1939 – M. Gillatt née Fowler

Old Laboratories – M. Gillatt née Fowler

Another photo from Margaret's album, above, is taken outside the school laboratories. It shows her class with their teacher, Mr Davies.

These highly inflammable laboratories were immediately behind Teddy Bear Cottage. Chemistry lessons took place to the left of the partition, while Biology and Physics shared the facilities on the right.

Another former pupil, Russell Warren Howe (1935-1942) sent the following recollections of life at the school while he was there:

"I came to CFS (we never used the L in those days) in 1935, ten years after the move from the Orphanage at Brixton. Only the Headmaster, Mr Parkinson (whom we nicknamed 'Plank'), the Headmistress, Miss Hutton and the Housemaster, 'Bob' Roberts remained from the Brixton staff. However, the Brixton regime was still very much in place.

For instance, we were not allowed out of the grounds except on Sundays, and then only under the control of a Master or Mistress, or a second year monitor or a prefect. In theory we were not allowed to go down to the village to buy tuck either, but because by then we had day-boys (and later, day-girls) we got round the rule by giving them money to buy tuck and doughnuts for us. We also nipped into Harbottle's confectionery shop illicitly on Sunday walks, since Harbottle's son was a day-boy and was anxious to have our approval.

Staff

The bedrooms at the Mansion were used as dormitories, while the 'boudoirs' on the first floor had become the Masters' bedrooms. Those on the second floor had become bedrooms for the Mistresses. The teaching staff were all celibate. In return for a comparatively low salary, they were lodged and fed, but were required to take on many extra duties unpaid.

Extra duties

Bob 'Froggy' Taylor coached cricket and trundled round the grounds with a machine painting white lines for the athletics tracks. He also organised trips for the boys to go to Paris.

Athletics Track – School Archives

Basil 'Kong' Rowland, and 'Jammy' Davis (his initials were JAM) coached rugby and taught life-saving. They also ran summer camps in Dorset or the Isle of Wight. Summer camps were popular, and sometimes as many as five Masters took advantage of this modestly paid holiday.

'Bob' Roberts taught the first form Religion. He was also responsible for Art in the whole of the Junior School and ran the weekly tuck shop. The shop worked on a 'bank' system, where we gave Mr Roberts pocket money from our parents and he deducted money from this when we chose our sweets. He also handled our mail, and allowed the seniors to listen to educational programmes on the BBC, piped in from the Masters' Common Room. Once, when the Brains Trust started to debate a listener's question about whether or not co-educational schools were a bit risqué, our transmission was mysteriously. and abruptly, cut off.

As well as his administrative duties, the Headmaster, Mr Parkinson, took the religious assembly at the beginning of the day, and the School Service in St Giles' Church on a Sunday where he was a lay reader. He also ran the Debating Society, where I came to know him best."

Russell Warren Howe left The City of London Freemen's School in 1942 to go to Cambridge, then joined the RAF to become a Spitfire pilot a year later. We continue his recollection of the war years at school in the next chapter.

chapter 14

WORLD WAR II

Russell Warren Howe's memories of school during the war years

"The key event in the lives of everyone in my age group was World War II. Like the children in John Boorman's film, 'Hope and Glory', our life was entirely changed by Adolf Hitler. At School, food rationing was introduced, and 'Bob' Roberts took over the task of Head Gardener in the pupils' new vegetable garden. He once told my parents he saw himself as a sort of Mr Chips. I suppose as a lifelong bachelor, the energy and love he put into the School probably reflected his desire for some sort of family.

The invasion of girls

The most interesting thing that happened in 1939, as far as we were concerned, was the arrival of the girls from the City of London School. They were evacuees, joining us because the Luftwaffe had started to bomb London.

Our buildings were too small to accommodate them all, so they were billeted to accommodation in the village, and only used the classrooms in the afternoons. Later they were all moved to Yorkshire, but for one term our four-hour morning became a five-hour session and we had sports in the afternoon. The senior forms (I was then fourteen, and in the Upper IV) were told not to sneak into the quadrangle during the afternoon to see who was sitting in our places, so of course we all did. Virtually all of us had found notes in our desks, and we wanted to see which girls had sent them.

Before the War, if a boy so much as touched the arm of a girl pupil, he was taken to the Headmaster to be disciplined and told his behaviour was depraved. Now, with the gramophone playing and planes droning overhead, we were suddenly being encouraged to dance the slow foxtrot (which involves close contact with your partner) with girls.

The War brought changes to the School and to the UK as a whole. 'Nemo' King was the first master to get married and live away from the Park. He even bought a car so he could commute. Mr and Mrs Parkinson did not learn to drive, so they did not have a car. More surprisingly none of the teaching staff had a bicycle, so they all walked up and down to the village.

By far the most unusual development for us during the War was our year of life in the basement, when the Battle of Britain began. On the first night we moved downstairs because of a bombing raid, I made the supreme mistake of persuading a group of friends to take refuge with me in the basement bathroom. We discovered you should never try and sleep in a bath that does not contain (preferably warm) water. The following night we joined the others on the floor."

John Pettman (1940-1947) recalls:

"My father was a member of the Honourable Company of Master Mariners. He died when I was a child and thanks to that decision taken by the Corporation so long ago, I was to become a Foundationer.

School was a strange new world to me. A bare Junior Day Room with large tables grooved deeply along the grain, liberally stained with ancient ink and pitted with dart, pen and knife scars. Nowhere comfortable to sit in the day-room, dining room, or class-room. A warm radiator was a luxury. In the dormitory no rugs, mats, carpets, curtains, blinds or pictures. Under each bed a rectangular basket for pyjamas by day and clothes by night.

Blackout

Blackout was achieved by closing the very efficient shutters. This was an essential part of the war-effort and two seniors had Blackout Duty and walked round the building each night. This seemed to need a special patrol of the corridor past the kitchens in the basement!

Food

Food in war time and immediately post-war was basic. An egg was a rare and wonderful thing. Fortunately the long loaves of bread we had were always excellent, otherwise tea, the main evening meal at 5.30, would have been dull indeed. Occasionally there was only bread and a blob of margarine as big as your thumbnail. Two or three times a week there was a spoonful of jam, and a bun on Wednesdays and weekends. We were allowed to bring in our own 'spreadables' which we stored in the servery. We kept jams and marmalade, precious because they were rationed, and Bovril, Marmite, fish-paste and blackcurrant puree, not rationed but still highly prized.

A dominant thought of boarders was food. During School Cert and HSC exams, the boarder candidates had special suppers from the date of the first exam to the last, with wonderful food like ham salad, new potatoes and apple pie. Consequently we all looked forward to exams. Also, we found the sickroom was a good place to be in winter. An open fire and an opportunity to make toast created a little holiday. That's how it was in those days. No biros, no television, no personal radios, no tape recorders, no computers and no bananas.

Classes began after assembly and most classes were in our own form room. We went back to the main house for mid-morning milk, then dinner with some of the day pupils. They were taking advantage of the rationing system, in which the School could claim extra rations as a catering establishment. Five or six dinners each week for a dayboy also meant his rations at home were saved.

Bomb casualties and damage at the school

On Sunday we went to our lovely little church, both morning and evening. The School provided the choir for Matins. In the winter of 1940 the heavy bombing started in London and I attended a grammar school in North Lincolnshire. When I returned to City of London Freemen's School the next spring, the gentle old Rector had lost his life to an aerial mine. This was a bomb floated down by parachute, which exploded at the surface with little of its energy dissipated into the soil, so it caused maximum damage.

A different kind of bomb, an HE bomb, fell in the School drive where it curves in front of the house. The crater it caused closed the drive for the rest of the war. A scattered 'butterfly' anti-personnel bomb got the school horse. Old Mr Whitlock, a bearded and occasionally smocked countryman of times long gone by, had used the horse around the school grounds, hooves padded for the cricket pitch.

Clothing

Some of us became rather scruffy in our weekday clothes as the war dragged on, as clothing was strictly rationed, but we always started the day with clean shoes. We cleaned our shoes with blacking, which came in large blocks we moistened with water. Some boys started buying their own, and sat discussing the relative merits of Cherry Blossom and Kiwi as they polished.

Sleeping in the basement

By the time I returned to the School from Lincolnshire in 1941, everyone slept down in the sturdily vaulted school basement in bunks. While down there, Jenkins, a bottom bunker, reputedly got bitten on the ear by a rat. He awoke one night from a deep dream to find a bloody pillow, and everyone was very impressed. When the Blitz period was over, we stopped going to bed in the basement, except when a siren went in the night and we hurried downstairs to the bunks clutching our rolls of blankets. Basement to top dorm was a long way back again for the little ones trailing their bedding in the morning. Class work did not seem to suffer unduly because of disturbed nights, but the staff on all-night duty had a harder time.

We had our share of the Buzz Bombs, with their harsh, echoing, motorbike throb. Then later in the war came the rocket bomb, for which there was no siren or warning. I was in a dorm in the back of the house when there was a bang and a tinkle, and almost every pane in the front of the building shattered. The huge bomb crater was in soft soil at the top of the avenue just short of the hard surface of Park Lane. Immediately opposite was the house of 'Chiz' Temple, the carpentry teacher and School carpenter, whose other duties included teaching us all to swim. He was quite deaf and slept peacefully through the whole thing, until Mrs Temple woke him with the news that half the house and most of his bedroom floor had gone. If the bomb had landed a few feet further south, he and his wife and his little blind dog would all have been killed.

Canadians in the woods

Canadian soldiers were camped in the School woods and in neighbouring woods towards Headley and their trucks were soon speeding along the previously quiet roads. It may be difficult for the young reader to imagine, but we saw few people and rarely saw a vehicle, so their arrival really caused a stir. Before that, the only vehicle to be seen was Mr Taylor's bicycle. From the School woods some of their lads would lean on the fence and watch the girls playing tennis. The girls were soon told they were not allowed to talk to them.

We played them at cricket and invited them into the School Hall for tea, which in summer could be lemonade crystals and water, a couple of slices of paste sandwich and a bun. Then came the away match, on the same pitch. Everyone wanted to play, umpire and score because there was an away tea in the woods.

They taught us to play soft ball and the soldiers left behind bats, balls and bases for us when suddenly the camp had to go. The district seemed empty without these good friends. We did not know at the time, but sadly many of our Canadians died in the Dieppe Raid.

The end of the War

As the war ended we celebrated with huge bonfires on VE and VJ nights. Travel was safe again and the head girl and boy were invited to the Guildhall for the presentation of the Freedom to HRH Princess Elizabeth. Many of us went to the Lord Mayor's Show and enjoyed refreshments in Gresham Hall. Rugby enthusiasts went to Twickenham. There was even a School trip to Belgium, though unfortunately we were based in a part where the locals would not speak French.

Conscription

Most of us who left School in the forties were called up, some to the fighting. We had two moving memorial services and tears were shed for Hedley Archer and Dennis Wager, the only chap I knew who actually wore a 1st XV cap. Both men seemed very close, Wager known to all, Archer because his brother Keith was with us.

For many of my contemporaries, post-war conscription meant two years of National Service. Miss Long's teaching in map-reading and theodolite skills went well in the Royal Artillery and at Mons Officer Cadet School, where I found that our Ashtead standards were high. I was one of two cadets chosen to meet a visiting Field Marshall, Montgomery of Alamein. A pleasant man with an easy manner, the first question he asked me was: "and where were you educated, young man?"

Michael Upton

"The War features in my School memories in a number of ways. Denis Wager, who had recently left to join the Navy, was killed in an air raid while on leave. The School attended his funeral in the Parish Church. Then there was Hedley Archer who was killed in a flying accident whilst training.

One day I remember Alan Payne coming in to School and describing how his road, in the Village, had been devastated by a land mine. And there was the amazing incident when 'Chiz' Temple, the School carpenter who lived in Teddy Bear Cottage slept through the explosion of a V2 bomb, which blew off the front of his house.

The first V1 went over the School to land on the Hoover factory in Leatherhead. We were in the old chemistry laboratory at the time and our teacher, 'Jammy' Davies said not to worry as it was one of ours. That was before the explosion!

Then there was the Stamp Club that 'Froggy' Taylor ran, where he sold mainly Australian stamps, a number of which I still have in my collection, to raise money to provide cigarettes for Prisoners of War. Froggy also ran a Cannibals Club, where those caught biting their nails were drafted into a group who had to weed the cricket table."

Evelyn Patterson

Evelyn Patterson née Mills (1947) was a Lower V pupil in 1944 and remembers Major Sissons, who had joined the staff to teach maths, giving the class a lecture on what to do if they heard a flying bomb (V1) or ack ack guns: "We were told to get under our desks to protect ourselves from flying glass and falling masonry. It made a great impression on us and after break, when we were in the chemistry laboratory, the guns started up. We all disappeared as one under the tables and

'Jammy' Davies, the Chemistry Master, stopped mid-sentence in the middle of his lecture. He was extremely annoyed until we explained."

Malcolm Fruin who left in 1951 recalls.

"My most vivid recollection of life in Ashtead was waking up at 5am on my twelfth birthday (Feb 15th 1945) with glass all over my bed. I was sleeping between the windows in 23 Dormitory when a V2 fell beyond the Cricket pitch and blew out all the windows in the building. The remarkable thing was nobody was even cut. The only casualty was the porter's dog."

Teaching at the School during the War

The following account is compiled from archive information and the recollections of staff teaching at the School during the war.

Before the bombing began

"At the outbreak of War, Ashtead was considered a relatively safe area, and so School was to continue as usual. The staff and some volunteer pupils returned on August 30th 1939 to fortify the Main building. This involved making sand-bags, filling them and then piling them against the windows of the basement. We also built a small sand-bag 'look-out' on the corner of the balustrade for the fire watchers. It took a couple of weeks, but everything was ready for lessons to start on September 12th." *'Tubby' Rowland*

Firewatching – 'Ashteadian' 114

The girls arrive

During the autumn term of 1939, the City of London School for Girls was evacuated to Ashtead Park. Mr Parkinson arranged the timetable so the City of London Freemen's School had lessons in the morning and games in the afternoon, and the evacuee girls had a sports morning and a working afternoon. The girls were placed in homes in the Village and the staff shared a house in Park Lane. It all worked very well during the 'phoney' war, the quiet time before bombing began, but once the blitz started and the village was hit, the girls' parents grew concerned. The next term, the girls were all moved up to Yorkshire. The City of London School for Boys was also evacuated and they went to join Marlborough College in Wiltshire.

Back at the School, for safety's sake, all the boarders were moved down into the reinforced basement to sleep. The girls had bunks in the room near the lift, and the female domestic staff, two teachers, matron and nurse were in the boot room, which is now the recording studio for the Music Department. The boys slept on bunks in the changing rooms, and the male staff in a room under the Men's Common Room, which is now the Headmaster's Secretary's room. The Domestic staff were housed in the wine cellar. The adults had camp beds, but this was the only concession to luxury.

Naturally, everyone was very safety-conscious, and so the staff had a lot of extra duties. The Master on duty slept under the stairs and the Mistress on duty had the bed nearest the door. As there were only two Mistresses at this time, it meant

Plane under attack – 'Ashteadian' 114

one night on and one night off. The Masters only had a duty every six or eight nights, because there were more of them. Duty involved a lot of fire watching, as the local Fire Brigade believed fire would be the biggest hazard.

"As Hitler had a big armoury of incendiary bombs, this was a real threat. The Fire Brigade tested the hose in front of the house and the fountain went over the cedar tree and on to the tennis courts. As the school obviously had a good supply of water, the Brigade warned us that we had very low priority on their emergency call-out list." *'Tubby' Rowland*

In the School Grounds

The Royal Norfolk Regiment arrived and stayed for a very short time. They were only there long enough for King George VI to review them on the rugby pitch before they moved out. Then the Canadians came, living under canvas in the lime avenue opposite the Main House. They were friendly and helpful, and always checked everything was all right after a bad raid. After the War, they presented the Bishop's Chair to St Giles' Church to mark their time in Ashtead.

Christmas 1939

"Over Christmas 1939, the Committee decided it was inadvisable for some of the children to return home, as they lived in high-risk areas. So we crept around filling stockings for them, and generally made it a very enjoyable time. We had log fires and a festive Christmas tree in the Senior Girls' Dayroom, now the Head's study. We could also take the children to the cinema and the pantomime. Luckily for them and us, the cook stayed on for Christmas." *Mary Rowland*

War time activities

As time went on, staff were being called up into the fighting forces. The first to go was the boys' Gym Master, Lt-Com. Joisce, who re-joined the Navy. A new project was started with parties of boys working in the kitchen garden under the supervision of Mr Rose. They even extended their efforts to start a potato field.

An article on aircraft identification appeared in the 1940 issue of the Ashteadian. Soon practically every child in England could identify the type and make of an aircraft from the ground, as it was vital to be able to identify enemy aircraft. There was also an article on stamp collecting, which became a favourite past time for the children, often cooped up in the basement for hours on end. In the autumn of 1940, the boarders sometimes managed tea and prep before the sirens went off, but often it was straight out of School and into the basement.

Staff wedding

July 1940 also saw a much happier event, the wedding at St Giles' Church of two members of staff, Mary Cooper and 'Tubby' Rowland. "On my wedding day, I had to travel up to Waterloo on the 8.15 train to escort the boarders meeting their parents for the holiday. Then I tore back to check on the caterers and get ready for the wedding. Later, as I walked out of the church, I saw all those boarders were back again with their mothers, greeting me along with the invited guests." *Mary Rowland*

The start of the blitz

When the blitz began, the children all went down to the basement during daytime raids, but once the flying bombs started falling there was not enough time. Instead, the first form children climbed under their desks while the teacher crouched down and read them a book to keep them happy. Everyone became very good at this routine and the teacher was often handed the book open at the right page to continue the story from the previous raid.

1940 went out with a bang as a bomb landed on the corner of the drive, leaving a crater big enough to prevent vehicles getting up to the House for nearly a year. It also sent up large lumps of chalk, some of which went through the roof of the Dining Hall. If the bomb had gone through the roof, all the people sheltering in the basement would probably have been killed.

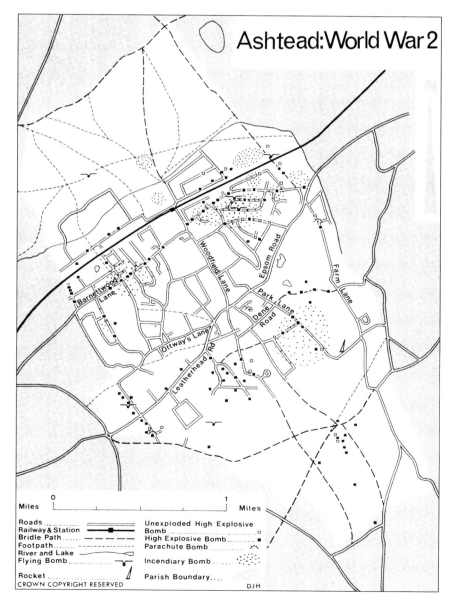

Ashtead: World War 2

Roads	Unexploded High Explosive
Railway & Station	Bomb
Bridle Path	High Explosive Bomb
Footpath	Parachute Bomb
River and Lake	
Flying Bomb	Incendiary Bomb
Rocket	Parish Boundary

CROWN COPYRIGHT RESERVED   DJH

Bombs in Ashtead – 'Ashtead' a villiage transformed

"This was the time when most of the incendiaries landed in the Park, and the staff were assigned to patrol in twos to watch out for fires. There was only one incendiary fire in the House, but several incendiary bombs landed behind the gym.

The butterfly bomb was another danger. These landed like an opened can of beans, and were dropped by the hundred. Despite their innocent appearance they were killers. If we found any, the police were called, and they were removed. We often saw the local constabulary walking in the Park looking for these unexploded bombs." *'Tubby' Rowland*

Back to the dorms

As the night-time raids eased, the staff and children were gradually allowed to return to their beds and only went down to the basement shelter when the siren sounded. The ones on the top floor were the most vulnerable, so a routine was established for them to get down there as fast as possible. "Me and my seven boys, aged about nine, would get up, put on dressing gowns and link up by holding dressing gown cords to walk to the basement. One day, to my horror, one of my 'links' was missing. I searched the School in panic and found the poor confused child had got his bath towel and washing things to go to the washroom." *Mary Rowland*

Casualties and Prisoners of War

Every Ashteadian recorded a number of sad losses as men failed to return from flights or were torpedoed. Others were officially reported missing, sometimes later found to be prisoners of war. Proceeds of the dance on Old Boys' Day went towards providing parcels of cigarettes and other useful items for ex-pupils in prisoner of war camps. In this Bob Taylor played an invaluable part, writing and sending parcels to ex-pupils on all fronts.

The Old Freemen's Association is fortunate enough to have some of the letters and cards our boys wrote thanking him and saying how they were coping with life in the camps.

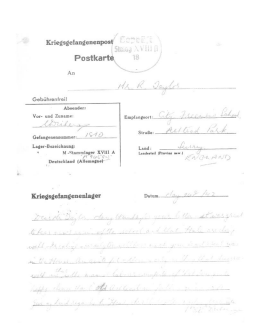

Card from a P.O.W. – Mrs P. Taylor

Card from a prisoner

In May 1943, Bob Taylor started collecting foreign stamps and establishing a fund to assist families bombed out of their homes in London. He also organised a series of fruit picking camps from the summer of 1942 until the Ministry of Agriculture dispensed with this essential service towards the end of the 1940s.

A photo of the fruit picking camp at Stoulton, near Worcester in 1946, which came from Keith Archer's collection. He left the same year.

Fruit picking 1946 – Keith Archer

Prize Day 1944

In complete contrast to Prize Days before and after the war, the occasion passed without a ceremony of any kind. The whole thing lasted only a quarter of an hour. For security reasons it was held on the North Terrace in the open air and only members of the School were present. Mrs Parkinson, the Headmaster's wife, presented the prizes.

Rations

In the war years, rations allowed to each person varied slightly from time to time. In 1944 the weekly ration for each person was two ounces (55 grams) of cheese and butter, two pints of milk, two ounces of tea, four ounces of bacon, eight ounces of sugar, one shilling and two pence worth of meat and one egg every other week.

Ration books were issued to everyone in the country. They contained marked squares showing the date and the type of food allowed, and the grocer or butcher would cut out the requisite section.

Clothing was also on coupons, which meant the strict rules on uniform had to be relaxed a little. The Governors decided Matron should keep 75% of the Foundationers' allocation and allow the parents the rest.

VE Day

Victory in Europe was celebrated with two days' holiday and a visit to Box Hill for the boarders. A huge bonfire, reinforced by incendiary bombs, brought a long-awaited conclusion to the war. Things did not return to normal straight away of course, and at the School many pupils managed without bedroom windows from February through to September owing to the slow progress on the repairs to the House.

Old Freemen's Day was a time for celebration with the return of ex-prisoners of war, but it also revealed the sad gaps left by those who fell in all parts of the world.

Staff and pupils who lost their lives in World War II

E Hedley Archer	John P O Bell
Alan C Boughton	A Keith W Brown
Peter B Brown	Philip J Buchanan
Reginald A Channings	Lawrence R Clark
Michael C Daniell	David H Edwards
Daniel H. Everett	Alan W K Foxon
Roger W G Fray	Robert H Godfrey
Patrick G Griffiths	A. G. Harrison
Alan Hunt	Edward Joisce
G Anthony Keeler	John F Kirk
Peter A Kleboe	Basil E S Knowles
Kenneth G Marsh	John D Owens
John Page	Wither G Price
Peter G Russell	Colin R Russell
J T Roy Sherriff	Eric Short
James D V S Stephens	Brian van Mentz
Dennis Wager	Sidney R Yeomens

A Memorial Service

The Old Freemen's Association held a special Memorial Service for the war casualties on 23rd November 1947 in St Giles' Church.

They decided to build a Clubhouse in recognition of the sacrifices their colleagues had made.

Mr Davies and Class – Alan King

Finally

In retrospect, it is surprising how well the School not only kept going, but also increased in popularity during the war years. All credit must go to those who kept it working during that difficult time.

Alan King's photograph c 1940 shows the disproportionate number of boys to girls. It also features 'Jammy' Davies, a Master remembered by his pupils with great affection.

Photo of 1st XV Rugby Team 1937-8 with Mr Rowland and Mr Parkinson – Alan King

Mr Parkinson retires

The summer of 1945 saw the retirement of Mr Parkinson. He was only the fourth Headmaster to be appointed since the School was founded in 1854, and had held office for thirty-one years, through both World Wars.

The Old Freemen's Association did not forget all he did for the School and in 1997 a bench was dedicated to his memory. Mr Rowland, who had taught with him, made the address and his son John expressed his gratitude to all the past pupils who had contributed to the memorial.

John & Jane Parkinson on the Parkinson bench
– David Harn

chapter 15

THE LATE 1940s TO 1950s

After Mr Parkinson retired, the School started the post-war period with a new Headmaster, GG Henderson. Other teaching staff returned as they were demobbed, each issued with an identical pin-stripe suit. The country began to flourish, and so did the School.

One of the first changes after the war was the amalgamation of the girls' houses, Wren and Gayer by the creation of the present House system of Gresham, Hale and Whittington. Mr Henderson had started a concerted effort to raise not only the numbers, but the morale and status of girls. Sadly he died only two years after his appointment, before he could see his efforts come to fruition. A successor, Michael Kemp, acknowledged the admirable work Henderson achieved in his brief time as Headmaster by ensuring co-education was adopted whole-heartedly.

"It took quite a considerable time but once equal numbers had been achieved this purpose was reflected in the deliberate maintenance of that balance of girls and boys on the School roll, which had risen from 220 in 1945 to 465 in 1971 (when his article was written) and still included Foundation scholars, thus fulfilling the School's original charter."

A rare photograph of Henderson is this one taken with the School Rugby XV 1945/6, kindly donated by Keith Archer.

The Obituary notice the School enclosed with the Ashteadian of September 1947 conveyed the sentiments of both staff and pupils.

"Mr Henderson was a forward thinking Headmaster who, in the short time he was in charge, made great improvements. He gained the affection of everyone he worked with, whether adult or child, and his death was a great loss to the School"

Henderson also introduced a proper library. Before he came there was a very small, well-used collection of reference books. He obtained a grant of £100 and a library was developed, classified by the Dewey system and housed in the Octagonal room. The service was later extended with boxes of books borrowed from Surrey County Library, which were brought out into the classrooms once a week for pupils to select and return. The system was kept up until 1951, when the first real library was created in the Headmaster's study (generously vacated by the then Headmaster, Mr Fielden).

Library/Livery Room – Jean Baumann

Ferndale Hockey Club Badge – Joan Cole

The Old Freemen's Association

In 1947, an important event for former School pupils was the founding of the Old Freemen's Association. Its aim was to maintain the connection between Old Boys and Girls and the School. Of course there had been several former clubs for past pupils. The first was The Hale Club, founded around1880 and named after the School's founder, Warren Stormes Hale. It was very much a male preserve, running river outings, visits to places of historical interest, whist drives and dances, and holding an annual dinner with the Lord Mayor as chief guest.

Then in 1914, the girls had set up The Ferndale Sports Club, named after Ferndale Road in Brixton, where the original School building stood. Miss Robins, the Headmistress, invited them to have the inaugural meeting at the School and accepted the post of President. The Club's main activity was hockey, played weekly on the School ground. It closed when the School moved to Ashtead.

In 1920 the newly formed Old Boys Club (called City Freemen's School Old Boys Association) joined with the Ferndale Club for a number of social events, chiefly dances and whist drives. The two societies merged in 1927 as the City Freemen's School Old Scholars Association, despite predictions from some intractable male members that the union would bring dire consequences. Mr Parkinson was its first President.

In 1928 the Ashteadian was circulated to members for the first time and an Association tie was introduced.

Then in 1929 the Association split again, owing mainly to the dwindling number of girls in the School. In 1938 The Old Girls club ceased to exist, so girls leaving no longer had any organised means of liasing through the School. However, the City Freemen's School Old Boys' Association, as it became, kept going.

Finally when Henderson became Headmaster in 1945, he oversaw the initiation of the Old Freemen's Association. The Association runs and maintains the Memorial Clubhouse, built in memory of former pupils and staff who lost their lives in the Second World War.

Conditions at the School after the war

Mrs Pauline Taylor née Dart

Pauline retired as Senior Mistress in 1975, and has vivid memories of her arrival at the City of London Freemen's School. "When I got to Freemen's in January 1948 as a new resident member of staff, I was appalled by the spartan conditions in both the staff bedrooms and the dormitories. I quickly bought myself a comfortable divan. But the eventual transformation of the girls' dormitories was memorable. In place of the one iron bedstead, one chair, one basket and no floor covering, there were new mattresses and blankets. Then small chests of drawers arrived to replace the baskets, and there were accompanying bedside rugs. It still was not Hilton standard but it was a vast improvement."

John R. D. Brown

"On my first day at School in January 1945 I had to take a mattress upstairs from the basement. The decision had been made to re-occupy the dormitories. Each pupil had only a bed and basket.

Later a Ministry Inspector required that we hung our day clothes on a chair overnight as dumping them in a basket on the dusty floor meant that they were never aired. The arrival of chests of drawers was regarded with curiosity. Everyone had a drawer to him or herself but had virtually nothing to put in it."

Photo of Tea in the Egyptian Room at the Mansion House – Pat Jenkins

The first City Visit

The idea of an annual visit to the City was devised to ensure that the pupils did not forget the School's links with London. The first visit was organised by Mr Fielden in 1951 and it was considered quite a feat to transport the 250 pupils up to the City. No-one taking part in that first outing could have imagined the problems presented by the numbers increasing to over 800.

It became tradition to set the annual visit in the autumn term. Classes visited places of interest in and around the City, then after a church service in St Bartholomew the Great, everyone had tea at the Mansion House. This itinerary has seen a few variations over the years.

The new block

The old science laboratories were situated in a wooden framed building behind Teddy Bear Cottage. The Chemistry Department was on the left and the shared Physics and Biology area was on the right. When the new block was built, the laboratories moved over there. The Domestic Science Department took over the old labs.

Old Chemistry Laboratory – School Archives

Guides at CFS – Veronica Ball née Taylor

Veronica Ball née Taylor (1953)

The Girl Guides

The increasing number of girl pupils included many readers of popular girls' adventure stories, all keen to experience outdoor life with the Guides. Veronica Ball (nee Taylor, 1953) built a secret 'camp' in the Wild Garden and asked Miss Dart, the Senior Mistress, if the girls could join a local Guide group, or even better, have their own company. As a result, 1st Ashtead Guides was formed in 1949.

David Bell (1950-59)

Prefects

"When I arrived at City of London Freemen's School in September 1950, I was being shown round 21 Dorm with two other new boy boarders, Tony Vissian and Nick Jeans, by the dormitory prefect. We were joined by some of the returning boarders, who referred to the prefect as 'boss'. It was a while before I realised they were not using a generic title for all the boarder prefects, but were actually saying his name, John Boss.

I soon learned there were five prefects in the Boys' Boarding House (then part of the Main House) and they had a room under the stairs on the right hand side of the entrance hall, just inside the front door. This small room was known as 'The Draughty Hole,' which apparently describes it well. Of course the prefects never kept the place tidy themselves. Every so often, one of them would go out and nab a couple of unfortunate junior boy boarders to do it.

On one such occasion, the press-ganged junior boys were clearing out accumulated debris from behind the radiator when they struck gold, numerous sheets of paper inscribed 'Labor omnia vincit' (Work conquers all) repeated hundreds of times.

These were the lines meted out as punishment by the prefects on any wrong doer, and the number of lines varied between 50 and 500, depending on the severity of the crime and the whim of the prefect. Obviously these sheets represented past labour by various boys and had been carelessly tossed behind the radiator when handed in. Once smuggled out of the 'Draughty' we put them to very good use as they were 'recycled' by future transgressors.

New Premises for the Prefects and the Headmaster

The Boy Prefects' room was later relocated to a partitioned section of the Junior Boys' Dayroom, and had a pleasant view of the tennis courts on the east side of the House. The Girl prefects had a matching room in the Junior Girls' Day Room. The change was due to the formation of a library in the Headmaster's study (now the Livery room), and the Headmaster subsequently moving his study into the 'Draughty.'

It seemed strange at the time, as the boarder prefects had moved to bigger premises while Mr Fielden had moved into the cramped 'Draughty' under the stairs. This state of affairs was finally remedied when the next Headmaster, Mr Kemp, moved into the Girls' Senior Day Room, where the current Headmaster has his Study.

Dormitory fun

While we were still junior boarders in 21 dormitory, one of our summer bed-time pranks was to arrange the mattress and bedclothes so that they formed a u-shaped 'tent'. We did this by tucking in the top sheet and blankets so tightly that they forced the mattress to flex into a 'U' with the bedclothes stretched tightly across the top. It could only be achieved with the occupant inside the bed while the others did the tucking in.

One evening it was my turn, and I was under the bedclothes exhorting them to greater efforts to obtain a really narrow U, when I suddenly realised that the merriment had ceased and there was a deathly quiet in the room. I cautiously peered out from my 'tent' and there was Mr Conway, the Master on duty, glaring down at me. I crept out and remade my bed under his stern gaze. It put paid to that evening's entertainment.

Lunch

When I arrived at City of London Freemen's School, the lunch plates were brought on large trays to the end of every dining table. Each plate would then be passed from person to person down to the centre of the table until everybody had been served. This procedure was repeated for desserts.

One of these desserts was tapioca pudding. Occasionally we found this gastronomic delight had such a remarkably sticky, sludge-like consistency we were able to pass plates of the stuff down the table completely upside down. The system later changed so the prefect at the head of each table was responsible for doling out the food.

Lunch was taken in one sitting in those days

The Dining Hall – John Burkes

The Boys' dormitories

The dormitories had bare wooden floors and no heating whatsoever. Before 1926, when the House was still privately owned, these rooms had fireplaces. Although the fireplaces themselves had disappeared, the marble bases still remained as part of the dormitory floor. A prefectorial punishment, especially in winter, was to make a transgressor remove his pyjama jacket and lie down on one of the marble slabs.

Not only was there no heating, but also the dormitory windows had to remain open, even in the depth of winter, so we got our requisite ration of fresh air. Getting fresh air was considered very important in the 1950s. However, our geography teacher, Miss Tebble, took the opposite view and at the start of her classes, she made sure all the windows were tightly shut. One of her favourite sayings was "Fresh air kills thousands daily".

A balancing act

When I was about 12 years old, in 23 dormitory, I decided to do an imitation of Blondin (the tightrope walker) by walking on the top bar of my bed head. I lost my balance and fell on to the bed, causing the springs under the mattress to burst apart, and the mattress to sag into the hole.

Not wanting to tell anyone in authority I had caused grievous damage to School property, I kept quiet and spent the next few nights uncomfortably wrapped around a huge dent in my mattress. Then, some days later 'Nobby' Clark (the School Engineer) came up to me and said: "I've repaired your bed – you should have told me the springs were like that." I couldn't believe my luck. He must have made a routine bed inspection and seen the wreckage. Truly a fortunate case of least said, soonest mended.

Responsibilities

It was customary for boarders to be given a position of responsibility for half a term or so prior to being considered for the position of boarder sub-prefect. One of these jobs was being in charge of ringing the School bell for the end of break times and for meals. Another was to collect the Dayroom newspapers each morning from Ashtead Village. As Bell is my surname it was inevitable I would eventually be given the bell ringing duty. It would appeal to Mr Bob Taylor's sense of humour. One day I was ringing the bell in the main House when I was suddenly surrounded by a large heap of rope. It had frayed and then finally snapped, a disaster of the first magnitude, as the bell governed our lives.

During the few days it took to repair the rope, I was reduced to ringing a hand bell on the North Terrace to try and summon everyone back to classes. Amazingly everyone still managed to get to class reasonably on time.

When 'Nobby' Clark repaired the bell pull, he took no chances. Instead of the usual rope, he installed a woven steel wire cable and I had no further trouble.

Scouts at CLFS – David Bell

The School Scout troop

Many of the boys, particularly the boarders, were members of the School Scout Troop, the 2nd Ashtead. The troop went away for a 10-day camp immediately after the end of every summer term. At one of these camps, each patrol was taken to a village some miles away, and told to walk back to camp using map-reading skills. Our group were left in the village where the parents of our patrol leader, Anthony Read, had spent their honeymoon, so we used up half the afternoon exploring the place.

By the time we got around to plotting our course back to camp we were beginning to feel tired and hungry. So when the footpath forked, our map-reading skills having deserted us, we decided to toss a coin to decide which path to take. Fortunately we chose the right one and were soon back at camp. Needless to say when asked to describe our journey back, we kept quiet about our un-scout like method of route selection.

Hair cuts

At some time during the latter half of the fifties, arrangements were made for the boarder boys to have their hair cut by Mr Hedges, the school porter, who lived in Teddy Bear Cottage. His salon was one of the old storerooms off the basement corridor of the Main House. In those days it led to the boys' changing rooms, but is now part of the Music Department.

There were the usual derogatory comments about pudding basin haircuts, but I think he did a good job and I often availed myself of his services. He was much cheaper than the barbers in Ashtead or Epsom."

Russell Schurmer (1960)

"Joining the Lower Fourth form in the mid fifties, most of my classes were taken in rooms other than my own form room. I found it very difficult to remember to consult my prep book every class, to make sure I had the correct materials with me. If I got the text and exercise books right, I would invariably forget my ink and my pen would run out.

Another thing that I recall of those halcyon days, was each year, around November, we made a visit to London to take tea with the Lord Mayor in the Guildhall. Of course we did not stand and have a chat with the eminent gentleman over tea and a sticky bun, it was just that he was present. Prior to the tea we visited somewhere of interest. One year we went to Bishopsgate Police

Form 1 at work in the 1950s – School Archives

Monday	Tuesday	Wednesday	Thursday	Friday	Saturday
Physics (Laboratory) (Mr. J. Rivett)	Free Period (Library)	Chemistry (Laboratory) (Dr. J. Allen)	Free Period (Library)	Mathematics (Room 18) (Mr. T. Conway)	Mathematics (Room 18) (Mr. T. Conway)
Physics (Laboratory) (Mr. J. Rivett)	Free Period (Library)	Chemistry (Laboratory) (Dr. J. Allen)	Mathematics (G.J.D.R.) (Mr. T. Conway)	Free Period (Library)	English (Room 9) (Mr. W. King)
Break	Break	Break	Break	Break	Break
Physics (Laboratory) (Mr. J. Rivett)	Free Period (Library)	Chemistry (Laboratory) (Dr. J. Allen)	Schol. Physics (G.J.D.R.) (Mr. J. Rivett)	Chemistry (Room 5) (Dr. J. Allen)	Current Affairs (Room 9) (Mr. B. Rowland)
Physics (Laboratory) (Mr. J. Rivett)	Scripture (Room 16) (Rev. D. Welsh)	Chemistry (Laboratory) (Dr. J. Allen)	Schol. Physics (G.J.D.R.) (Mr. J. Rivett)	Free Period (Library)	Current Affairs (Room 9) (Mr. B. Rowland)
Lunch	Lunch	English (Room 17) (Mr. W. King)	Lunch	Lunch	Lunch
Free Period (Library)	Mathematics (Room 16) (Mr. T. Conway)	Lunch	Mathematics (Room 16) (Mr. T. Conway)	Free Period (Library)	
Mathematics (Room 16) (Mr. T. Conway)	Mathematics (Room 16) (Mr. T. Conway)		Free Period (Library)	Gymnastics (Gym.) (Mr. E. Burkes)	
	Free Period (Library)			Mathematics (G.J.D.R.) (Mr. T. Conway)	
	Gymnastics (Gym.) (Mr. E. Burkes)				

David Bell (1950-59)

A Sample Timetable for the 1958/9 School Year – David Bell

89

Station where I got locked in a Black Maria. After the visit we went for prayers at St Bartholomew's Church then on to the Guildhall."

Ros Robertshawe

A teacher from New Zealand, Ros enjoyed her first spell of teaching in Ashtead Park so much she came back.

"I first began teaching in Ashtead in January 1956. Mr Fielden was the Headmaster. Mr Taylor, was the Senior Master and Boys' Housemaster and he lived on the premises on the first floor. Miss Dart (later Mrs Taylor) was the Senior Mistress living in a small room on the ground floor just along from the Mistresses' Common Room (now the staff Dining Room).

The Octagonal Room – School Archives

The boy boarders lived on the first floor of the Main House, which they reached by a staircase to the right of the entrance hall, whilst the girls were on the second floor and used the main staircase. The Changing Rooms were all in the basement. The boys' changing rooms were accessed from the stairs under the main staircase, while the girls used the back stairs and had their lockers and showers off that end of the basement corridor.

The library was off the octagonal room, which became the staff mixed Common Room in 1973, and after that the Livery Room. What is now the Headmaster's Study (from 1984) was the Senior Girls' Day room, which was used for prep and recreation. All the classrooms were in the Stable Block, except for Art, which used the Conservatory. There was no swimming pool or proper hall for concerts or shows. We had to use the Peace Memorial Hall for the School plays.

The Senior Girls' Day Room – School Archives

In 1958, the last year of my first session, the New Block on the upper quad was opened and there were two science laboratories and about six extra classrooms. Form I stayed where it was in the Stable Block and the room next door became the music room, from which the acoustic tiles on the ceiling fell down with monotonous regularity, until they found the proper glue.

At that time not all the Masters had cars, and I just had a bicycle, which was very useful. Wednesday was a half-day with Sports in the afternoon, but we worked on Saturday mornings with some Sports in the afternoon. Derby Day was the exception. The School was given a half holiday as it was considered the day pupils would not be able to travel home because the buses would be full of race-goers.

Many things changed during the six years I was away, but one thing that did not change was the City Visit. Unfortunately for me, the same forms went to the same venue each year, so I got to see the Tower repeatedly. We then went for a service in St Bartholomew the Great Church before tea in the Mansion House, or occasionally a Livery Hall."

Dame Sybil Thorndike

The School was fortunate to have Anthony Casson as one of its boarding pupils as his grandmother, Dame Sybil Thorndike, the famous actress, took an interest and was known to have given readings to the pupils, especially the boarders on several occasions. The Sixth Form also had the benefit of a visit backstage after a London performance in which she performed with her husband Sir Louis Casson. The family connection went further when her son designed the swimming pool.

A piece of history

School in 1944 – "Ashteadian" 116

Squadron Leader FG Fray (1937) wrote in February 1991:

"I was a pupil at your School before the last war. My leaving bible is dated July 1937, when the Headmaster was Mr Parkinson.

"I joined the Territorial Army in 1939 and on returning from Dunkirk in 1940 I transferred to the RAF for pilot training. Commissioned in January 1942, I spent the rest of the war flying Spitfires on special duties doing Photo Reconnaissance over occupied Europe as far afield as Besslie or Stuttgart. Sometimes if we had spare film we ran our cameras out over familiar 'targets'. Now, all these years later, I have been looking through some of my memorabilia and have found this picture I took of the old School back in 1944."

chapter 16

EVENTS SURROUNDING THE 1954 CENTENARY

Let us recap the main events of the first one hundred years 1854–1954 in a time line.

1852   Foundation stone laid at Ferndale Road, Brixton.

1854   Opening of the City of London Freemen's Orphan School on 28th March. Headmaster is Rev W Brownrigg Smith. School roll: 32 boys, 18 girls.

1855   First co-educational lessons by visiting Drawing Master – for reasons of economy.

1856   100 pupils on roll.

1858   Two pupil–teachers stay on to help teach.

1861   School leaving age raised from 14 to 15.

1863   150 pupils.

1866   Death of Rev WB Smith. Appointment of Marcus Tulloch Cormack as Headmaster.

1880   Staff of Headmaster and three Assistant Masters. Headmistress and two Assistant Mistresses. Visiting Masters for French and Drawing. Visiting Drill Sergeant and Bandmaster.

1889   Resignation of MT Cormack after serious troubles at School. Appointment of RE Montague as Headmaster. 100 boys and 65 girls on roll. Pupils entered for Cambridge Junior Certificate.

1890s Appointment of Miss Robins, Mr Lowe and Mr Roberts.

1903   Appointment of Miss Hutton – later Senior Mistress.

1914   Outbreak of WW1. Appointment of WW Parkinson as Headmaster.

1916   Mixed classes due to shortage of staff during the Great War

1918   Senior pupils entered for School certificate. Leaving age raised to 16.

1919   Inspection by Board of Education after WW1 recommends the School is moved to more suitable premises. School Committee decides to move the School out of London, to admit fee-paying boy pupils and to raise teachers' salaries to attract more highly qualified staff.

1922   Miss Robins dies.

1923   Inspection and subsequent purchase of Ashtead Park by the Corporation of London.

1926   School moves to Ashtead Park at Easter. School roll 47 boys, 42 girls.

1927   School renamed The City of London Freemen's School.

1928   *The Ashteadian* No.1 published. School Roll 82 boys, 34 girls. Appointment of Mr R Taylor, who finally retired as Deputy Head in 1968.

1931   Inspection by the Board of Education reflects the need for strengthening the curriculum.

1932   Mr Lowe retires after 33 years' service. Appointment of Mr WH King, who retired as Senior English Master in 1973. First School visit to Europe – Belgium. Miss Hutton retires as Senior Mistress.

1854 Foundation Trophy containing the original plans of the School in Brixton

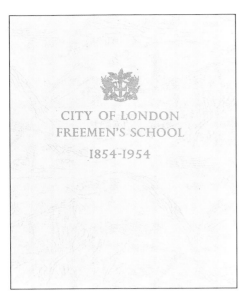

The Commemorative Book – School Archives

An Aerial View of the School – School Archives

1933   Fee-paying girls admitted. Appointment of Mr BE Rowland.

1939–1945 World War II. Mr Parkinson retires in 1945 after 31 years as Headmaster and Mr Henderson is appointed in his place.

1947   Mr Henderson dies unexpectedly.

1948   Mr Roberts retires as Second Master – the last link with Brixton. Mr Fielden is appointed Headmaster. The Guides are founded.

1949   March saw the official founding of the 2nd Ashtead Scouts CFS.

1951   The first City visit - intended to remind pupils of the School's connection with the City.

1954   Centenary celebrations

The Commemorative Book

To commemorate the Centenary, the School produced a well-illustrated paperback, which you can examine in the School archives.

Pupils remember

Kate Pittom née Little (1947-1954)

Kate had gained all her qualifications for training at The Middlesex Hospital, London but was too young to take up her place. She persuaded her parents to let her spend a further year in the 6th form and was appointed Senior Girl Prefect.

"Without the pressure of exams I had a really good time playing a lot of sport and achieving my colours in hockey, netball and tennis. I was girl House Captain of Whittington too, so it was great that we won the Cock House shield again. I also took part in the Dramatic Society production of The Winslow Boy at Ashtead Peace Memorial Hall.

There was still time during the Easter holidays to help at an international two-week holiday for young people from France. It was organised by Mr Bob Taylor at a camp in Seaford, Sussex. The venue was a primitive, barracks-like establishment, which was not very clean. For the first and only time in my life I picked up impetigo. However, it was good fun hosting the French students, practising our French and helping them with English. We took them to London, Rye, the beach and the South Downs.

Back at School for the summer term John Lambert (Head Boy) and I were co-editors of The Ashteadian under the direction of Mr Wallie King, and we began to put together the Commemorative edition of the magazine. A series of photographs of the School at work and play were commissioned to mark the Centenary.

Various senior pupils, including me, were allowed to forsake lessons while we posed in shots depicting serious study in the Library, walking around the grounds and playing sport. My nine year-old sister Susan helped too, sitting at a desk in the front of the First Form wearing a painting overall in an Art Class.

Preparations for a special Prize Day also went ahead and I remember practising very hard for a display of formation marching and movement to music, which was to take place in front of the Main House after Prize Giving. To this day I never hear a Sousa march without thinking of that display, organised with such enthusiasm by the gym mistress Miss Crawford.

John Lambert and I were also included in the middle of a large Centenary photograph with all the staff, the Aldermen, the Sheriffs, the Governors and the Lord and Lady Mayoress of the City of London. (I used to show that photo to my children Elizabeth and Richard when they became pupils at the School.)

That Prize Day John and I were invited for strawberries and cream in the marquee with the City representatives, which was a great honour. My sister, as the youngest girl in the School, was chosen to present the bouquet to the Lady Mayoress. Altogether it was a very memorable day on which to receive my Leaver's Bible. About ten days later term ended with the tear-jerking hymn at Assembly: "Lord dismiss us with thy blessing, all who here will meet no more."

After everyone had gone, and the School had fallen silent, I can remember proof-reading the Centenary Ashteadian, in the Library with John and Mr King before cycling sadly away. I realised how fortunate I had been to have enjoyed my school days so much and that last Centenary year in particular."

The Service of Thanksgiving

Centenary celebrations continued to the end of the year. Dr Wallbank conducted a Service of Thanksgiving at the Church of St Bartholomew The Great on October 5th 1954. It was the day of the City Visit, which was followed by tea at the Mansion House as the guests of Sir Noel and Lady Bowater, The Lord Mayor and Lady Mayoress.

The Centennial Dinner

On November 12th, there was a further celebration, the Centennial Dinner, at the Guildhall, in the library, for past scholars of the School. A trio of students from the Guildhall School of Music entertained the guests. The Old Freemen's Archives holds a complete list of guests, along with a copy of the menu.

Work on the Memorial building

Also during the Centenary year, work continued on the Memorial building; these photos show the progress being made.

Photo of the Memorial Building – O.F.A. Archives

Finally in 1955, Major Wells, the Chairman of the School Governors performed the official opening ceremony of the Old Freemen's Memorial Clubhouse.

However, by 1958 membership had increased to the point where a larger Clubhouse was needed, and fundraising began so the original building could be extended.

The Careers Panel

In November 1957, the Old Freemen's Association sent out a letter asking members to help the School by giving careers advice to any pupils interested in following a similar career path. Members with all kinds of jobs responded, all willing to give their time and expertise for the benefit of the next generation of school leavers.

The Opening of the New Block

There are very few photographs of the complex always known as the New Block, but aerial view shots show it lying behind the Assembly Hall, roughly where the Haywood Centre building now stands. It was in use from September 1957, but the official opening did not take place until November 29th.

The Ashteadian

The Magazine of
The City of London Freemen's School

Cover of "Ashteadian" No 91 May 1975 gives good aerial view.

Official opening group – School Archives

The School, parents and visitors assembled in the quadrangle formed by
the New Block and the gymnasium to await the arrival of the Lord Mayor, the
Freemen's School Committee and the Headmaster, Mr Fielden. Everyone was
delighted with the new complex, as it offered not only modern classrooms, but
up-to-the-minute science laboratories.

Design Workshop - School Archives

Science Lab - School Archives

chapter 17

THE SCHOOL IN THE 1960s

Mr Fielden

Mr Fielden was Headmaster from 1948 to 1963. A quietly spoken, rather shy man who rarely raised his voice, he worked hard for the good of the School. His time as Headmaster saw many changes, including the extension of classroom accommodation in the New Block, which enabled the School to expand to two streams from Form 2 upwards. He also initiated holding morning assembly in St Giles' Church, instead of the Dining Hall. Mr Fielden actively supported the Scout troop. The photo shows him as Quartermaster, peeling potatoes at Scout summer camp in Highcliffe near Bournemouth. He retired in 1963 and a new Headmaster, Michael Kemp, was appointed in 1964.

Mr Fielden – Centenary Booklet

Mr Fielden at Camp – David Bell

Ros Robertshaw

My return 1964 –1967

"When I came back to teach at the school again in 1964, Mr Kemp was in his second term as Headmaster. Philp House was built with John Lansdown installed as Housemaster, and Gordon Vowles as his Assistant. There was also a Matron to oversee the boys' laundry, cleaning and other duties.

We were still performing the School play in the Peace Memorial Hall. The comedian Harry Secombe's son, Andrew, attended Freemen's for a while in the 1960s and I had the task of teaching him and his contemporaries Religious Education. Harry attended at least one of our carol services in St Giles' Church whilst Andrew was at the School.

Meanwhile the girls took over the first and second floors of the Main House. Sylvia Bek was in charge and I was her assistant. We had flats on the top floor. Unfortunately they discovered dry rot and we had to vacate our flats for treatment to take place.

There was also a Matron for the girls' department and a new purpose built sick-bay in Philp House with a fully trained nurse in attendance. The boy and girl boarders now really met only at mealtimes or in the classroom. As the School had grown from around 300 pupils to something like 400, there were three sittings at lunch.

Derby Day was no longer a holiday, nor was Wednesday a half day. Staff timetables now included a half day off in addition to other non-teaching periods to compensate for teaching on Saturday mornings.

There were House Prayers and Assemblies once a week with special boarders' services in Church most Sunday mornings. When the Lord Mayor and his entourage visited for Prize Day, it was held in a marquee, as the School still did not possess a proper Hall.

Tug-of-War – School Archives

Athletic sports and the Inter House tug-of-war, with the Masters and pupils yelling their heads off for their team to win, were great days. In fact sports facilities were expanded in the 1960s to include two new hard tennis courts, a netball pitch and a hockey pitch, with a new rugby ground and two composition cricket nets opposite the Old Freemen's Clubhouse.

The trophies were presented on the steps of the Italian Garden."

Central Heating

With the change in the boarding arrangements, central heating was installed in the Main House. Unfortunately this led to some of the panelling splitting in the Dining Room and Library (Livery Room).

It was around this time the Headmaster took over the former Girls' Day Room as his Study. The room's lovely stucco work was further enhanced by paintings borrowed from the Guildhall. The adjoining Conservatory had now become the Music Department.

Gordon Vowles

"I was appointed to the staff at City of London Freemen's School as Head of Chemistry after an interview with the Headmaster, Mr Fielden, during the summer term of 1963.

When I arrived in September of that year, I found that Mr Fielden had unexpectedly retired and Robert Taylor, the Senior Master, was in charge of the School.

My first impressions were mixed. The post was residential and I had been led to expect I would be provided with a bedroom and sitting room. In fact my accommodation consisted of a small sparsely furnished bedroom (destined to become the Housemistress's bathroom a year later) and a partitioned share of the boys' washroom. My sitting room was in fact the Men's Common Room!

Scouts

On arrival I had found a letter awaiting me from the Scout District Commissioner, Mr Geoffrey Gollin. He had heard that I had agreed to take over the School Scout Troop and was sure that I would take the troop to the annual St George's Day parade at the end of the week. Summoning the scouts to meet me for the very first time, it soon became clear that this idea was not popular and in fact caused a near riot. I remember a patrol leader said, "I'm afraid we are not a very religious troop, sir."

A very disorderly group of boys attended the parade on the Sunday and harsh words were necessary. Despite this unpromising start I was to continue an association with the troop for six years as Scout Leader and many more as Treasurer.

The Chemistry Laboratory and Lecture Room were brand new having been opened at the end of the previous term. A new boys' boarding house was in course of construction in which I had been promised a flat.

At that time the boarder girls lived on the second floor of the main house with the Housemistress, Sylvia Bek, and her assistant Ros Robertshawe. The boys occupied the first floor with Mr Lansdown as a non-resident Housemaster. Mr Lewis and I lived on the premises. A duty room was provided in which non-resident staff slept overnight when on duty."

John Lansdown

John Lansdown had arrived at the City of London Freemen's School in 1946 after military service, which included the Dunkirk evacuation and the Normandy beaches. For many years he served as Assistant in the boys' boarding house under the Housemaster at that time, Robert Taylor. In 1957 he took over as non-resident Housemaster. John and his family lived in Avenue Cottage. The gate in the curtain wall will still be remembered by boarders of those days as 'Lansdown's Gate'.

The arrival of Mr Kemp

1964 was to prove an important year in the School's history as Mr Kemp arrived to make his mark as the new Headmaster. Under his leadership the School developed and improved to such an extent that he was later elected to the membership of the prestigious Headmasters' Conference (1984).

Mr Landsdown & Mr Lewis – George Lewis

During the summer holidays, much work was carried out in the Main House. As the girls were to take over the first floor vacated by the boys, their new accommodation was extensively remodelled and redecorated.

A completely new floor was installed in the lofty kitchen to provide for a flat for Miss Proctor. She was the first Lady Superintendent and had responsibility for all domestic and catering arrangements. This was before the School employed professional caterers. The maids' quarters were altered, as there was more space on their floor now the Sanatorium had been moved into Philp House. The changing rooms in the basement were also improved, whilst the ground floor rooms which had been used as boarders' day-rooms were adapted and redecorated to provide a new Headmaster's study, a new Art Department and a Music Room.

Philp House

Philp House was officially opened in 1964. It was named after Ian Philp, a widely respected Governor who sadly died before he could see the realisation of the splendidly equipped modern building for which he had fought. In the autumn the boy boarders moved in to the excellent facility, with underfloor heating throughout, four large dormitories, day rooms, lounge, hobbies room, drying room and various service rooms. Flats were provided for the House Matron and Assistant Housemaster. The building included a four-bedroom Housemaster's residence and a Sanatorium with wards, surgery and Nursing Sister's flat. A new oil-fired system was constructed under the building, which provided heating for the whole School.

Philp House – School Archives

John Lansdown moved in as the first Housemaster. He and his wife lived in the Housemaster's residence adjoining the boys' accommodation. It was he who planned all the detailed arrangements and routine for the boarders in their new home. The successful structure he devised was to remain for many years.

Philp House foreign tour

In the Easter Holidays, 1966, John Lansdown and I ran the first Philp House foreign tour. With eight boys and two cars, loaded with camping equipment, we made for Geneva via Reims and Dijon. Here we received wonderful hospitality at the home of Mr Thomas of the International School who was formerly on the staff at Freemen's. From there we went to Turin via the Mont Blanc tunnel and on to the Italian and French Rivieras, Fontainebleau and Paris. It was so successful and enjoyable, we ran similar tours in the following years.

Further changes

In 1969 Saturday morning school came to an end. From then on, the Boarding House staff were responsible for their charges for the entire weekend. In 1972 five day boarding became an option.

I took over the House in September 1975. At the same time Mr Jones arrived as Assistant Housemaster. For three years, before moving on to Stowe School, he gave invaluable help. While with us, he successfully produced *Androcles and the Lion* with a cast of twenty-six boarders, as well as helping with several boarders' weekends to the West Country.

Following the intake into the School in 1978 of 30 extra pupils at 13+ it was decided that the two day-rooms in Philp House would be used as teaching rooms. It was at this time that a small portion of the largest room was partitioned off to provide a study room for three boarders.

In 1979 the numbers in the House had increased to 52 boys and I was keen to provide more privacy and suitable study facilities for those working for external examinations. That year the Governors agreed to the conversion of one dormitory into six study bedrooms. With the existing studies this enabled 12 boys to have the use of study bedrooms with a further 9 being given more private facilities for study.

I handed over as Housemaster to Mr Steptoe in 1982. It had been a busy, tiring but satisfying seven years during which, with the help of the Assistant Housemasters, Sister, and Matron, the House thrived. There were very few disappointments, with most boys fulfilling expectations and taking a full part in the life of the School.

The academic side

During my time (1963 – 1989) the School numbers had increased from 385 to 650. The Junior School was built in 1987/88 accounting for over 100 pupils of this increase, mainly 8 and 9 year olds. In 1963 Biology, Physics and Chemistry had one laboratory with a shared Lecture Room. There was a single laboratory technician for the whole School. By 1989 each of these subjects had two laboratories and there were now three laboratory technicians. Additionally there was a new laboratory for Electronics. In the same period of time examination results had improved beyond measure with excellent results all round year after year."

Prize Day 1968

This year, the Junior forms were sent to the gymnasium and had the service relayed to them, which gave more space to everyone in the marquee. The printed programme was enlarged to include details of school activities.

With the end of Saturday morning classes, holidays were shortened slightly so tuition fees could stay the same, and Saturday mornings at School were only used as punishment time for miscreants. Robert Taylor, The Senior Master, retired at the end of the Autumn Term.

Mediterranean Cruise – Mrs P. Taylor

Mrs Pauline Taylor née Dart, Deputy Head 1948-1975

Educational cruises

"The School's 1967 cruise to the Baltic included Russia. Pupils visited Leningrad and took an overnight train to Moscow. It was a particularly useful trip that year as the History 6th were studying the Russian Revolution for Advanced level.

I remember the School group attracted much attention as we insisted on School uniform being worn in Russia. 'Colours' blazers were especially noticed. Some of the girls in that year's blue striped summer dresses were given flowers.

We filed past Lenin's body in the Mausoleum in Red Square, and even the liveliest of our party were subdued. We also asked, much to our guides' annoyance, to be taken to a 'functioning' church on the Sunday. There we were made very welcome at a Russian Orthodox service.

1970 to the Mediterranean

This was an interesting trip but it did not make as much impact as our trip to Communist Russia. It was a glorious summer and we spent much of our free time sunning ourselves on deck, which is where I took this group photograph.

Those educational cruises were highly organised, and at the final Prize Giving, C.L.F.S. was prominent. I don't think that Clive Parminter has ever forgiven me for writing his name so poorly that it appeared on the prize programme as Olive.

Both our trips were on the *Nevasa*, which was later scrapped in the Oil Crisis because as an elderly, but very well equipped British India vessel, she burnt too much oil. The Falklands War ended these educational cruises, when the last vessel handling them, the Uganda, was called up as a hospital ship to the War zone."

Headmasters' Conference

In 1984, Mr Kemp was able to get Freemen's accepted into the prestigious Headmasters' Conference, which of course, was a great boost to the School.

Mr Michael Kemp, Headmaster 1964-1987

Mr Kemp very kindly sent these three reminiscences of his time at Ashtead.

"Woodman — Spare that Tree"

Wych Elm and props – School Archives

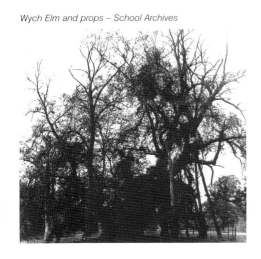

"Ashtead Park is renowned for the splendour and variety of its trees, exhibiting prize examples of all the trees of northern Europe. Many of the tall timbers provided local landmarks – like the noble Cedar tree – until the 1987 storm created such destructive havoc.

One tree had the distinction (so it is said) of having provided cover for the Anglo-Saxon Witan, a local government, which met a thousand years ago to deliberate on local affairs. This tree was the Wych Elm, which stood on a raised woody bank some 30 yards in from the modern north entry to the Park in Rookery Hill. Its slender branches survived because they were thinned out, allowing strong winds to pass between them without causing further damage. The trunk was frail and penned inside a dilapidated iron fence. The fence was a signal to everyone they should treat the tree with a respect appropriate to its age and grandeur and not to interfere with it.

When the School moved down from Brixton in 1926, some of the seniors found a new use for the Elm, in the shape of a thicket of foliage, which when viewed from the outside provided cover for the illegal (hence doubly attractive) environment for enjoying a quiet puff uninterrupted.

The Headmaster's Study claimed a commanding frontage to those who came to take advantage of the smokers' haven, and indeed a careful inspection of the elm tree after lunch on most days would reveal a thin spiral of smoke coming up from the screen of laurel bushes.

There it was that, sadly, the Wych Elm came to the end of its days. The removal of the laurels showed the ancient worm eaten timber. The old tree was thought to be resting its tired limbs on some supporting planks, but in fact the props ended some inches below the trunk.

So having braved so many storms, the tree finally had its fate decided by nature, and was spared the woodman's axe."

The actual site of the Wych Elm was just inside the School gates, if entering from Rookery Hill, and on the left hand side. The ground all along the Rookery Hill fence was subsequently levelled, so the site is now well and truly buried.

All Change in Main House

All Old Freemen who worked in the former Library (now the Livery Room) will know how handsome that room was, with its blocks of open shelving and very fine morocco leather, and will recall how only senior pupils were allowed to work there. Those who made use of this facility were firmly directed by the Head of Sixth Form and knew to make the most of this invaluable asset. By the 1970s the Library had grown, with gifts and donations, to about two thousand volumes. The bookcases could hold no more and something had to be done.

Taking time to consider possible ways and means of adding to the books and making them more accessible to all the pupils, I was delighted to see that beneath each bookcase was a set of four wheels. They were clearly mobile. I considered whether we had more extensive accommodation for them elsewhere in the School and decided we had. And we could also revise the role of different rooms to match up to a new library plan.

One problem remained. How to move the books and shelving to their new location adjacent to the Covered Quad (now part of the Sixth Form Common Room). Working to a tight budget we could not hope to bring about the necessary room changes. Then I thought of a solution. We could call upon our lively and muscular pupil battalions to do the job.

After careful briefing, and with due care and effort, the old Library moved from Main House, while the desks from rooms 6 and 7 were removed. By 4pm that day, thanks to the united effort of pupils and staff, the re-arrangements of the fittings had been put in hand.

The rest followed smoothly with the re-cataloguing of the books on the Dewey Decimal system by the efficient Mrs Knock, and by the devotion of Mrs Sears, who in due time became our first full time Librarian.

Second Library – School Archives

Walnut Tree – T. Riley

This undertaking was made possible by the joint action of the whole School and a fine day.

It is a lovely day tomorrow

It was one of those clear bright days when birds are nesting and bees buzzing with the promise of Spring. School children were pouring out of classrooms and labs, chattering and laughing as they moved in lines to the top of the Lime Avenue. When they reached the Avenue, a scattering of staff led each group to take up places in form order near the Old Freemen's Clubhouse. The sharp-eyed pupils noticed a small tree lying with sacking round its roots.

After a minute or two the Senior Staff gathered round a large City gentleman and I stepped forward to welcome Sir Thomas Kingsley Collett. Popular and renowned as an Alderman, he was also a Governor of some forty years, and a good friend to the School. He was a big man in every sense.

Taking the tree from the waiting Head Gardener, he wasted no time in placing and settling it firmly in the ground. From the shape of the leaves it was clearly a walnut. It was being planted to reinforce the connection between the School, the City and the Old Freemen.

There was one more task to be done. Sir Kingsley admonished the pupils to pay close attention to one instruction:

"The tree is for the School until the nuts appear on its branches. Then you must remember that the nuts belong to me."

As they turned and headed for the Main House the classes passed close by the walnut tree and perhaps a few thought of the School's historic niche in this new link with the Corporation of London."

The Lord Mayor's Prize Day Procession accompanied by Mr Kemp

The Lord Mayor's Procession – School Archives

Beatrice Somers née Watling (1967)

"One of the things I appreciated most about being a pupil at CLFS (though probably more in retrospect) was the staff. In the summer of 1967, 'Froggy' Taylor and 'Fanny' Dart took us on a trip to Norway, Sweden, Denmark and Russia – a trip I will never forget. They not only sacrificed their holidays so we could make the trip, but they also made it so enjoyable.

I remember going to the hotel in Moscow early in the morning after spending the night on the train from Leningrad, as it was then called. We all needed to freshen up, and there was only one room and one toilet for all the girls and staff. Fortunately Miss Dart's coolness and unflappability saved the day. It was on that same trip we managed to queue-jump while waiting to see Lenin's tomb, and saved ourselves several hours of unnecessary waiting.

I also remember Hardanger Fiord, where it was too rough for anyone to go ashore and a sailor fell overboard.

Another member of staff who went out of her way to reward the girls who held positions of trust in the boarding house was Miss Bek. She took the Head Girl of the Boarding House and the Boarding Prefects for a Chinese meal at the end of the year. The year I went was the first time I had ever had Chinese food and I really appreciated it.

Breaking rules

We weren't always as well behaved as those in authority thought we were. When I was in the Upper Sixth, and the Derby Fair was up on the Downs, a party of us snuck down the fire escape, over the King William Gate, and up to the Fair. The helter-skelter nearly proved my downfall as I suffered a very nasty burn on my right arm, which of course I did not dare report. I had an exam the next day, and just had to struggle through it!

It is a wonder more damage was not done to the library when I was at school. We had our bathrooms directly overhead, and it was common practice to turn on the taps, think of another job that needed doing, and come back to find the bath overflowing. The water would land on the lovely old table and we became quite proficient at re-polishing it. Having to repair the damage we caused was the punishment meted out every time.

Continuity

In spite of all the new buildings and other changes, there is still a sense of continuity for us Old Freemen. The part of the School that made me most nostalgic when I visited was the Girls' Boarding House. Naturally over the years there have been a number of changes to keep up with current boarding school standards, but I still found it recognisably the same."

chapter 18

EVENTS IN THE 1970s

The Committee changes

The School had been controlled by the Freemen's School Committee of the Court of Common Council since its foundation. On January 15th 1970 this Committee came to an end, to be succeeded by a slightly smaller Board of Governors, with Deputy Harry Duckworth as Chairman. Similar Boards were set up for the two City of London Schools, and together the three boards formed an Education Council, intended to co-ordinate and determine the welfare and life of all three schools.

Keeping our links with the City

Seven Senior Prefects from The City of London Freemen's School were invited to attend the ceremony when His Royal Highness the Prince of Wales received the Freedom of the City. Nowadays most of the old privileges of the Freedom (see chapter 1 for details) have disappeared and the Corporation presents the Freedom as a mark of high distinction for exceptional services to mankind. It is still the highest honour the City has within its power to bestow, and decisions to confer the Freedom are taken only by the Court of Common Council.

Monica Brown (1971)

Monica wrote this account of the prefects' special visit to the Guildhall.

"At 11 o'clock on Tuesday, 2nd March 1971, we took our seats in the Gallery at the West End of the Guildhall. The ceremony was due to start at midday, so until then we sat mesmerised by the people arriving. I remember the predominantly fashionable colours were purple and green. There was an orchestra playing and BBC cameramen were busy adjusting equipment, all adding to our enjoyment.

Once the Lord Mayor had taken his place on the dais, the principal guests were received individually. We recognised many of them immediately: the Prime Minister, The Attorney General (who was also our local Member of Parliament), Sir Alec Douglas-Home, the Lord Chief Justice, Mr Maudling and Mr Wilson.

When the guests were all seated the Lord Mayor moved in procession to the porch to receive the Prince of Wales and Princess Anne. Shortly after twelve, the procession made its way up the Guildhall to the dais. Everyone's eyes were on Prince Charles as he walked beside the Lady Mayoress. He looked strikingly handsome with a tan from his recent trip to East Africa, and wearing the uniform of a Colonel of the Welsh Regiment. I remember thinking he needed to put on some weight as he seemed a little on the thin side.

The ceremony began with prayers, then the Principal Clerk to the Chamberlain read the Declaration of the Patrimony Vouchers testifying Prince Charles was the Son of Prince Philip and was born in lawful wedlock.

The Worshipful Company of Fishmongers presented the Prince, and he signed the Freemen's declaration and the Roll of Fame. His Royal Highness spoke in a clear voice, making a speech that was both amusing and serious, and held everyone's attention throughout.

The National Anthem was played, and the ceremony was over. The principal guests accompanied the Lord Mayor to the Mansion House for lunch. The other guests were given lunch in different parts of Guildhall. The prefects from the three City Schools were served with a delicious three-course meal in the Livery Suite.

Unfortunately five prefects then had to rush straight back to School to take a Use of English Examination. Major Duckworth took the remaining pair of us round the archives of the Guildhall where we were shown a First-Folio of Shakespeare's plays, and a first edition of Sir Thomas More's *Utopia*. We were also shown the delicate work needed to repair old manuscripts.

It was both a memorable and enjoyable day for the seven of us. We felt very fortunate being able to witness a small part of history being made."

Mr Burkes – Portrait by George Lewis

Lord Mayor on Rope Bridge – "Ashteadian 86"

Other events in 1971

1971 was a good year for sport, with three girls representing the county at hockey and three boys at cricket. The Junior Orchestra won first prize in the final of National Youth Festival of Music, and two senior staff members, Pauline Dart and Robert Taylor, got married. Meanwhile, George Lewis arrived at the School as Head of Art.

1972 Mr Burkes retires

1972 saw the retirement of Edgar Burkes, a teacher at the School since 1939. He was a popular man who gave tremendous service to the School in many ways. He always attended Old Freemen's Day with a handful of photos in the hope that one or more of his ex-pupils would be able to identify themselves. His family very kindly donated a number of these photos to the Old Freemen, together with his portrait painted by George Lewis, which hangs in the Memorial Clubhouse.

Five day boarding

September 1972 saw the introduction of five day boarding. It gave an alternative to the previous arrangement with only one free weekend each half term

1973 – The Assembly Hall

Officially opened in June 1973 by the then Lord Mayor, Sir Hugh Wontner, the Assembly Hall was designed to cover everything from theatre, cinema and concert hall to providing badminton courts. All this is made possible by 'bleacher seating' which can be folded up swiftly into the wall.

Wallie King retires

During the opening of the Assembly Hall, the Headmaster announced that Wallie King was retiring after 41 years teaching English and Latin at the School. He had also coached athletics, rugby and cricket for many years and played for the Old Ashteadians (later Old Freemen's) 1st XV before the war.

In May 1934 he became editor of *the Ashteadian*, a responsibility he held for 39 years, during which the magazine trebled in size. He also ran the Literary, Debating and Dramatic Society.

He organised summer holiday camps, and after the war, harvest camps, fruit picking with Mr Taylor and Mr Rowland. Sharing responsibility with Mr Taylor, he went with School parties to Paris and to Koblenz. He was held in great affection by his pupils.

Wallie King had another claim to fame: he was the first married Assistant Master, and had to have permission from the Committee in 1938 to marry and live 'out'.

1974: Tubby Rowland retires

Tubby Rowland joined the School in 1933, teaching Geography and History (and later, Economics). Taking part in numerous sports activities and helping to organise School trips abroad, he also oversaw School swimming and life-saving award classes right up until 1972. He married a fellow teacher, Mary Cooper in 1940.

In the fifties he became Sixth Form Master, and he and his wife organised visits to theatres and concerts. Whittington House thrived under his leadership and was twice Cock House in eleven years, in 1957-8 and 1968-9. In 1961 Whittington won every competition.

A staunch Christian, he helped to take the Boarders' Services. He also started Community Service in the School, which involved camps for deprived youngsters and annual visits from Whitechapel children.

Mr King – Portrait by George Lewis

Teaching Geography and Economics up to his retirement, the School had to appoint two new members of staff to replace him. Between them, Tubby and Mary, who spent nine years on the staff, contributed half a century of service to the School, and above all else are remembered for their kindness and hospitality.

Mary died in 1994 and the Old Freemen's Association planted a tree in her memory at the front of the House, just outside what used to be the Mistresses' Common Room. Tubby died in 1996 and the Old Freemen planted a garden outside the Clubhouse as his memorial.

Tubby and Mary Rowland – Keith Archer

The Freemen's School Association

The Freemen's School Association was founded in 1974. A committee of parents and staff, including the Headmaster, Mr Kemp, it was formed to help raise funds for extra equipment for the School. Among other fundraising activities, the FSA revived an old custom and started up a Tuck Shop. It was run by volunteers and sold sweets to the children at morning break times.

The Swimming Pool

The Swimming Pool and the Assembly Hall were built with money raised by the pupils, parents, teachers and the Corporation of London. At the opening ceremony in 1973, the new swimming pool was described as a "25metre pool, with a twelve-feet deep end, housed in a vaulted hall of light pinewood. Daylight enters through timber mullioned windows comprising the far end of the building, which faces the Park." The pool brought swimming to the forefront as a sport at the School, and also provided an incomparable recreation facility.

The following report written by **Felicity Martin** is about a typical fund-raising event held in 1970. It originally appeared in *the Ashteadian* no 81.

The Swimming Pool walk

"As part of the School's effort to raise money for the Swimming Pool, a sponsored walk was held on September 20th, one of the clearest and sunniest days of summer. There were two routes, one for the juniors, and the other for the seniors, middle school, and the more ambitious juniors. The turnout of pupils, friends and dogs was so tremendously large and everybody was so eager to begin, the start was more like a riot in Grosvenor Square than a walk for charity.

The fifteen-mile route led first to Langley Bottom, where some of the more energetic walkers, obeying a notice at the edge of the track, embarked on a canter. From the checkpoint at the end of this stretch, the walkers cheerfully proceeded on road, until the sign posted 'Bridleway to Headley'. Here they rapidly became less cheery, realising it was not exactly a bridleway, but more a bramble-covered track. However, the spirit of determination was soon revived as Mr Cook, the leading member of staff, hacked a path through this jungle in a manner any Christian missionary would be proud of.

On emerging, cries of joy were uttered as the scratched, bleeding and thirsty walkers saw Mrs Kemp and Mrs Brumby invitingly holding out glasses of orange and lemon squash. Greatly refreshed, the walkers started the longest section of the walk, four miles. This led over Mickleham Downs, where, despite the description of landmarks, general instruction on the route sheet, and the guidance of Mr Vowles, many more foolish members of the School managed to get lost.

Those who eventually emerged found themselves, to their relief, at Burford Bridge, over halfway through the walk. From here the rest of the walk was along the by-pass, and later, the main street.

This, the most agonising part, was almost as painful to watch as to walk. Hundreds of bedraggled walkers either staggered along as if they were lost in a desert, or, following the example of those at the front of the walk, trotted back in the hope of getting out of the sweltering sun more quickly.

The shorter legged juniors tackled their nine miles with the same courage as everyone else. Part of their walk followed the senior route, but then took a different way through Headley, to come back via Tyrells Wood and Thirty Acre Barn.

So, by lunchtime, despite all difficulties encountered, most of those who set out had returned exhausted but rejoicing, having raised £1,137 for the Swimming Pool Fund. This was much better than expected and was possible only because of the determination and endurance of the walkers, and much more importantly the planning, supervision and encouragement of Miss Dart and the rest of the staff."

The Swimming Pool – John Keeling

A big drawback of the Swimming Pool was it only had one changing room, difficult in a co-educational school. The boys had to leave by the rear of the building and run across a courtyard to the back of an old laundry room they used as a changing facility, nick-named 'the ice box'.

Later, the pool's staff room was enlarged and converted into a proper changing room for the boys, complete with shower. At the same time the stairs to the balcony were taken into the porch area and the entrance door was moved to stop it causing a draught directly into the pool every time the inner door opened.

The 50th Anniversary in Ashtead Park in 1976

In 1976, the Headmaster, **Michael Kemp**, wrote this short piece for the School's 50th anniversary at Ashtead. It shows what a forward looking man he was and heralds the expansion of pupil numbers the School needed to survive.

"This anniversary takes full meaning as a milestone along our way, and from this vantage point in time we must look ahead to see the shape of things to come. Any worthwhile school is constantly developing. We are ready to grow in size, and in the climate of 1976 we have little choice but to do so, or stagnate and die. If this seems melodramatic, evidence may be seen on all sides of the ideological and political assault not only upon Independent schools as such, but on the educational philosophy they represent, while the swelling tide of inflation washes round their foundations.

A modern co-educational school of some 450 with a 6th Form under seventy strong is limited in the courses it can offer, the competition it can provide and the activities it can sustain. From an economic standpoint the savage rise in rates, costs and salaries must mean a fierce increase in fees, or a larger body over whom to spread the charges.

In view of this, the recent decision by the Governors, with the concurrence of the Court of Common Council, to provide for expansion over the next five years is both timely and courageous. Initially, provision will be found from within the present facilities, but a new laboratory and other developments are envisaged in due course. Despite pressures and problems, our prospects in 1976 are bright."

Jeremy 'Jok' Harle (1970-1979)

"It may be that my rose tinted spectacles are thicker and more opaque than most people's but I am pretty sure I had a great time at School. My year had a reunion in September 2000, some 21 years after we left City of London Freemen's School in the summer of 1979. After racking our brains for a while, we came up with a list of 77 pupils who had, at one time or another, been in our year. Then, after a great deal of effort, we managed to contact 45 of them and some 34 attended the reunion. Pretty good statistics, I thought. They demonstrate what a friendly, together bunch we were and still are.

The reunion held a surprise for all of us. The School was no longer exactly as we remembered it. For some reason, we felt strangely outraged. Despite the many and exciting changes the School underwent during the seventies, it was the people that really made our schooldays. The running of the School and its development were, by and large, constant in our lives and we did not consider it much at the time.

Looking back, and being a 'fat boy' of my year, my mind turns firstly to food. School meals were like something out of 'If' (the1968 film, starring Malcolm McDowell) or Harry Potter's Hogwarts. Pupils were seated at long tables with senior folk at the head and us poor menials at the bottom of the table. The food was brought to the table in large dishes and served out from the upper echelons then passed down to the 'grubs' at the lower end. Of course, brussel sprouts were easy to come by, but of chocolate pudding and sauce we had to make do with the mere smell. Food fights were rare but not unknown. Flicking semolina from a large spoon was somehow irresistible. I always did rather well when liver was served, as I actually liked the stuff. About 1974, new cafeteria style catering arrangements came in, and we started having 'sittings'. Mealtimes degenerated after that.

My failing memory says that at about the same time the School Swimming Pool and new Assembly Hall were built. The swimming pool was (and is) a great school asset but I missed the days of going to Epsom Public Swimming Baths for the annual gala. My brother (who was a pupil in the sixties) reports that in the days before my time, the Lord Mayor would attend and throw coins in the pool for pupils to dive and collect. That may even have happened in 1970; I can't be sure.

Also the old cricket nets that used to stand opposite the Old Freemen's Clubhouse were obliterated when a vast amount of very stony soil was deposited on them to make a new level pitch area. Now I do not want to boast, but my personal contribution to de-stoning was significant to say the least. I had no fewer than eleven 'On Reports' in one term and they all had me picking stones for an hour after school. The end of term reports sent to our parents used to list the number of detentions, on-reports and distinctions we had received. As I used to fake my father's signature on them, I had to tell him that '11' was a simple mistake that anyone could have made and that it should have read '1'. My father was either very gullible or very forgiving.

The Assembly Hall was a mixed blessing, I felt. It contributed greatly to social life at School with all the dances we had there. Many a torrid romance, that I fondly imagined but never actually took place, featured the new hall. But, alas, Prize-giving Day was never the same when the School did away with the big marquee tent erected on the hockey pitch behind the new block each year. Well, we called it the New Block, but I guess it is the 'gone block' now. Ah, the New Block. Taking off our shoes whilst waiting for Biology class and 'skating' down the polished wood floors of the corridor.

The new Assembly Hall was also used for the Drama Society evenings – occasions that allowed us free rein to lampoon the teachers. I am quite sure that the productions I was involved with were far and away better than any others. Harping back to food, a change for the worse was the closing of the school tuck shop. A sad day indeed when the mid-morning break no longer had us queuing for black-jacks and fruit salads. Time for a cup of tea and a plain chocolate digestive I think. Thanks for your time. Memory Lane is a great place to visit but I would not want to live there."

Sarah Jury (1971 to 1980)

"The things I remember from my first year at the School are the Assembly Hall and the Swimming Pool being built. From outside, the Assembly Hall was just like a large yellow cube, and it's nice to see attempts have now been made to make it more aesthetically pleasing. By contrast, the Swimming Pool would not have been out of place at a luxury Caribbean resort. Jumping off the top diving board, I think it was 15 feet high, was a feat that required buckets of courage for a ten year old who was not very athletic. I can still feel the chlorine up my nose!

The Assembly Hall – John Keeling

I was surprised to see the New Block (as we knew it) had gone when I visited. In our day it was much pleasanter than the old quadrangle area. At least the toilets were. The junior toilets in the Stable Block had creosoted floorboards and they had a pungent smell.

The Tuck Shop was next to the old Physics Laboratory. I remember one girl claimed the School lunches were so disgusting (by that time they were actually quite good) that she lived on shrimps and black-jacks from the Tuck Shop.

I was lucky enough in Form I to go on the last City Visit that included tea at the Mansion House, rather than the Guildhall Crypt. Those sickly cream cakes must have taken ages to clear up where we accidentally dropped them and squashed them underfoot."

Della Panton née Gover (1972-1980)

My first day - September 1972.

"We all had to assemble in the Dining Hall as the new Assembly Hall did not open until later in the year. I sat next to a girl called Katherine Gaitonde, whom I first met when we were taking the entrance examination. Next we were ushered down to a group of buildings called New Block, where room 16 became our classroom. Our Form Master was Mr Hancock. By this time we were sitting in alphabetical order and I was delighted to find myself once again next to Katherine. I do not recall much about the lessons but I do remember in the afternoon we were the very first class to use the brand new Swimming Pool.

City visit

My first City visit made a big impact on me. We were invited to tea at the Mansion House and there was a strict rule we had to eat everything on our plates. Unfortunately some of the bigger boys casually dropped food they didn't like on the plates of us smaller ones. They looked so big and important that we didn't dare argue.

The opening of the Barbican

I was fortunate enough to go to the official opening of the Barbican where several members of the Royal Family were present. I remember being surprised the Queen was so short, and how easily she and the Duke mixed with the crowd. Prince Charles came over to me and borrowed my camera. Unfortunately he fiddled with it and broke something so it never worked again!

In the Upper IV, I had a teacher who did not like me and I felt the same way about him. By then I was best friends with Sarah Banfield. I was attracted by her great sense of fun. Our form room was in the Stable Block, right next door to the book room. Sarah and I were passing when we spotted our teacher inside and almost without thinking Sarah suggested locking him in with the books. I agreed, but felt very guilty when she was put on report and I was not punished for helping her.

The seventies were a period when the IRA were very active and the School was believed to be a possible target. I remember at least three or four occasions when the whole school was evacuated to the middle of the Rugby pitches while checks were made in all the buildings. Unfortunately the bomb scares always seemed to be on the coldest days.

Once the fire alarm went off when smoke was seen rising from the guttering above the covered quadrangle (now the walkway of the sixth form block).
It turned out one of the seniors had thrown a cigarette butt out of the sixth form common room window and instead of dropping to the ground, it had wedged in the gutter.

Perhaps my most lasting memory of my time at school is when I joined the choir and we sang in St Paul's Cathedral at a service to celebrate 50 years at Ashtead, with Alan Davis as Choirmaster".

chapter 19

THE 1980s

An Old Freeman joins the Board

In 1983 Robin Eve (1943-1951), a Livery Member of the Chartered Secretaries, was the first Old Freeman to be elected to the Board of Governors.

The Old Freemen's Association

Judith Alsopp (1973) was the first Old Girl to be elected Chairman of the Association in 1983. This year was also the FSA's 10th anniversary, and they marked the occasion by using the funds raised to buy the School a minibus and some computer equipment.

The School on TV

Meanwhile the School had been approached by Thames Television, and on September 1st 1983 a television crew arrived. Thames Television was filming a Science Fiction Story by John Wyndham, and wanted to use shots of a cricket sequence and film of a classroom to complete the serial. The money raised from their visit was added to the School Bursary Fund.

Plans for a new Junior School

In 1984, the School asked outside consultants for advice on development. The consultants' report suggested lowering the age of entry to allow eight year olds in, fitting in with Surrey L.E.A. Middle School age range of eight – twelve year olds. Subsequently the Headmaster, Michael Kemp, put together plans for a new Junior School.

Back on TV

In 1985 the School was used again to film the Benny Hill Show during the summer holidays. Michael Stilwell, the School Bursar, was given the job of supervising the filming. Being a keen photographer, he took lots of photos

Benny Hill – Michael Stilwell

of everything going on and made up a really interesting album. The facia of houses built in the Old Freemen's Car Park looked realistic enough for an audience to see it as a street.

This was also the year the first School video was made by Martin Hearne. The 'premiere' was at the FSA annual general meeting.

1986 — Ashtead's Diamond Jubilee

By 1986, the School had 550 pupils, 40 teachers and a sixth form of around 100. A core of teachers remained at the school all their working lives, but many now wanted to extend their experience by working in other establishments. More staff changes brought in new ideas and ways of managing subjects. And there were more specialist teachers, something almost unknown in the fifties and sixties. Best of all, this was the year the Board approved the idea of starting a new Junior School, and planning permission was approved 1986/7.

The Queen's Sixtieth Birthday visit

This account is from Ashteadian No.111

The Head Girl, Sarah Goulder, and Deputy Head Boy, Martin Breadmore, enjoyed a rare privilege on the Queen's Sixtieth Birthday, April 21st. At the invitation of Mr Eve, Deputy Chairman, who was on the City's organising committee, and in company with the Head Girl of the City of London Girls' School, they drove from Guildhall to Buckingham Palace in a line of splendid limousines. There they delivered the City's loyal greetings expressed on a large birthday card, together with a huge basket of flowers. After returning to Guildhall, they participated in the ceremonial cutting of an enormous birthday cake in Cheapside.

Special events at the School

Naturally Ashtead's 60th anniversary was marked in a number of ways. Even the gardeners wanted to make it a special occasion and planted out a City Crest in the Italian Garden.

Crest in the Italian Garden
School Archives

A Guildhall Display

George Lewis, Head of the Art Department, arranged for copies of various historical school pictures to be mounted on board and displayed at the Guildhall to celebrate the 60 years at Ashtead. The exhibition was displayed again years later in the Geography Department for the celebration of 75 years in the Park.

"Views"

This was a special magazine of the pupils' writing, liberally illustrated with photographs, brought out in the Spring of 1986. It was printed from Mr Hearne's early IBM word processor, as a prototype of camera-ready production for the *Ashteadian*.

A Barbican Concert

An ambitious musical event was held in the spring term – a full-scale public concert in the Barbican Concert Hall with the other two City Schools. This was to happen over the next decade just twice more at five year intervals.

Special edition

A special Diamond Jubilee edition of the *Ashteadian* was produced, with a spectacular aerial shot of the Park on the cover. Celebrating the many achievements of the School, it also recorded the sad deaths of former teachers Robert Taylor and Wally King.

The Finale of the Diamond events

The Ashtead Diamond Jubilee celebrations ended with a bonfire and fireworks. Reported to be a magnificent display, it was a fitting close to the year's events.

Keeping links with the City – the Hale Dinner

Maintaining the School's links with the City, around twenty pupils (mostly from Hale House) were invited to attend the Hale Dinner, as dinner guests of the Tallow Chandlers in their Livery Hall on Dowgate Hill. They were there to honour the memory of the School's founder and benefactor Warren Stormes Hale.

The pupils were shown some unique Hale memorabilia, and ate a sumptuous meal with members of the Livery and their ladies. They learnt a great deal about Warren Stormes Hale during the course of the evening.

1987: Michael Kemp retires

The Headmaster, Michael Kemp, retired in 1987 and David Haywood was appointed in his place. During his time as Headmaster, Michael Kemp had seen the School through many significant changes, and standards had risen spectacularly. He will always be remembered for his remarkable energy and depth of knowledge, as well as his many achievements on behalf of the School.

Michael and Helen Kemp – School Archives

David Haywood - Current Headmaster

Hurricane damage – Paul Dodds & George Lewis

A new Headmaster

David Haywood was appointed Headmaster and took up his post on 1st September 1987 having been Second Master at Dauntsey's School in Wiltshire for 5 years. He brought with him considerable experience in the day to day running of a co-educational day and boarding school of similar ethos, as well as experience in the highly academic atmosphere of King Edward's School, Birmingham where he had previously been Head of Geography for 8 years. A distinguished sportsman he is a graduate of Jesus College, Cambridge and achieved a 'double blue' in cricket and soccer. Together with his wife Meta and two young sons he moved into the Headmaster's House in Rookery Hill. In 2000 the Corporation sold the house and the family moved to Deer Leap on the far side of the cricket field in front of the Main House.

The Hurricane

The day after a successful City visit, Friday 16th October 1987, Ashtead Park was a scene of terrible devastation. Overnight a hurricane had toppled many of the trees and left a litter of branches from those that had survived. As many as ninety trees were lost and an equal number badly damaged. A programme of tree planting was quickly implemented by the Headmaster with Corporation assistance – some 1100 saplings were planted in the next 12 months, including a new Lime Avenue to the front of Main House. Great emphasis on woodland management and conservation procedures were a further positive outcome. This was in 1987 just 6 weeks after David Haywood's arrival.

The Ashteadian

A new feature in the *Ashteadian* of 1987 was where former pupils, who left four years ago, reported on their progress since leaving School. This standing feature was enjoyed not only by their contemporaries but also by the staff and other Old Freemen. The Magazine reported that Mr Robin Eve (1951) was elected as Chairman of the Board of Governors, the first former pupil to achieve that honour.

David Haywood, the new Headmaster, started out by reorganising the playing fields as work began on the new Junior School. He also formally and reluctantly disbanded the 2nd Ashtead Scout Troop because pupils had stopped showing any interest in it.

1988: The Opening of the new Junior School

The Spring Term 1988 saw the first Livery Day, when forty visitors from different Livery Companies were welcomed to the Park as a gesture of thanks by the newly appointed Headmaster for all their support to the School. It also saw the fund raising and planning for the first ever World Rugby Tour by the squad. However, the major event of 1988 was the opening of the new Junior School in September.

As a tribute to Michael Kemp, who put so much effort into the planning of this part of the School, the Governors under the Chairmanship of Duncan Lawrence decided that the building should be called Kemp House. It was officially opened by the Duchess of Gloucester on Wednesday 19th October 1988, and increased the School roll by over 100 pupils.

The Junior School – John Keeling

Floodlit Astroturf

Another huge success in 1988 was the new all-weather-surface; a floodlit astroturf pitch for hockey and tennis, replacing the old gravel surface in the woodland to the south-east of the Main House. It improved the reputation and standing of the School hockey teams, which was already high, and generated even more interest in the sport. In the following few years the playing fields were also realigned and landscaped on both sides of the Main House.

Duke of Edinburgh Award Scheme

The 1980s saw a continuing rise in popularity for the Duke of Edinburgh Award scheme, with many pupils gaining awards. The scheme involves many courses such as First Aid, Police Service, Life Saving, and Safety in the Home and includes quite challenging expeditions.

1989

The death of John Cole on January 28th 1989 was a sad occasion for the School. He had taught English and Latin at Freemen's since 1978 and for ten years was Chairman of the Debating Society. The Senior School was closed for the afternoon of the funeral and many pupils, former pupils, colleagues and former colleagues were amongst the congregation. He was remembered for his kindness and his sparkling wit.

Changes

Gordon Vowles retired after teaching Chemistry at the School from 1963 to 1989. Paul Terry, the popular Music Teacher, also left to start his career as a text book publisher, consultant and examiner.

The Children Act 1989 led to some changes at Philp Boys' Boarding House. The old fashioned dormitories were replaced with more modern smaller units

Mr John Cole – Martin Hearne

Mr Gordon Vowles – "Ashteadian" 115

for between two and four pupils. The layout of the girls' house in the Main House could not be changed because the building is listed, but staff levels were increased for both boarding houses.

David Way (1988)

David is a musician, so it is not surprising he remembers the musical aspects of School life most vividly, especially as he was fortunate enough to obtain a Musical Scholarship to the School.

"I enjoyed playing in an ensemble of violin, cello and piano with Trevor Pratt, who went on to become Head of Music at Manor House School, and Jenny Janse (1986). We took part in School concerts and on one occasion gave a recital in the Guildhall Library as part of the fund-raising for the Music Department.

As a violinist I particularly recall the String Ensemble, which was coached and directed by Frederick Campbell, a very flamboyant person who was also congenial and very generous. He wore flared pinstripe trousers and rode a red moped. When Mr Campbell left, Stephen Dinwoodie was appointed and he was a complete contrast. There was certainly no messing with him!

The Musical Director at that time was Paul Terry and the Music Department owes him a terrific debt of gratitude, as he was the one who got all the staff involved and made them feel part of the School. For instance, he asked them to act as backing to the School Choir and selected the different musicians to sit on the panel of judges for the House Music Competition. Paul also conducted the orchestra and brought them to greater heights.

Another member of the Music Department was Charles Stewart, the Choirmaster, and an accomplished pianist and organist. I met him again when I was playing for the Bournemouth Symphony Orchestra and we turned up at Winchester Cathedral for a rehearsal before a recital. There was Charles looking very grand in his position as Precentor to the Cathedral. Rather different from the Master who would play the viola in the orchestra when they were short of players. I remember he once turned up to Choir Practice in a kilt, which was his right as a Scot, but produced a feeling of glee amongst the singers.

Another interest of mine was the Debating Society under the direction of Martin Hearne. The debate I remember most was on the topic 'This House believes School is an outmoded institution.'

It certainly produced a lively discussion."

Simeon Lando (1988 – 1993)

"Theo van Dort and I started at the School on the same day, which coincided with the launch of the first School coach run, starting in Surbiton and ending in Ashtead. The drivers were an odd bunch and it wasn't long before we decided to have a pretend fight on the coach. The driver didn't see the funny side and we nearly got banned from using the coach in our first week. In the end we both used the coach, and had the distinguished honour of being promoted to coach prefects, until we passed our driving tests a good few years later.

I fear the lessons which had most impact on my memory are probably the ones in which I was least accomplished. Spanish at GCSE level wasn't taken very seriously as the poor teacher had almost the entire rugby team in her class.

She found it very difficult to control us and tried the strategy of moving us around as soon as she walked into the classroom, but it wasn't all that successful.

On one occasion I was sitting at the back of the room and the boy next to me pretended to fall back and hit his head on the wall. I immediately started to play the concerned friend and the teacher rushed over to us obviously expecting some serious damage. He just sat up and said 'April fool'. I seem to remember it happened in the autumn.

Rugby was a major part of my school life and I was fortunate to have gone on tour to both France in 1990 and Canada in 1992. I remember Dick Best coming to coach us after he had been appointed England coach and giving us a training session from hell. I also remember the rugby squad cheering when I grew a lot bigger than Bill Deighton and he decided to join in a training session. After lifting him on my shoulder, I dumped him on his backside.

My main claim to fame was compiling the first yearbook in 1993. I cannot believe we left City of London Freemen's School ten years ago and that I am soon to celebrate my second wedding anniversary."

chapter 20

THE 1990s

New playing fields

In the 1990s Independent Education was changing rapidly. Almost 70% of new parents had not been through the Independent system themselves and so their choice of school was based on practical and economic factors. Value for money incorporating quality teaching and excellent facilities became their yardstick. Nothing was taken for granted although pupils' happiness in a friendly well run school was very important. As a result Independent Schools became more competitive and realised the need to market themselves. David Haywood was only too aware of this changing pattern and knew that to survive and keep the school successful he must improve the facilities whilst maintaining the high quality of teaching and family ethos that characterised Freemen's.

After overseeing the construction of the Junior School and the floodlit all weather Astroturf pitch in his first year and the subsequent re-landscaping of all the playing fields, he developed a bold and ambitious plan for expansion and re-development that would require considerable funding throughout the 1990s. His vision for the future included the almost complete rebuilding of the Senior School on the site of the existing, largely single storey, buildings of wooden construction which had outlived their useful life. Although he was well supported by the Board of Governors, it was not easy to obtain the necessary planning permission but eventually his enthusiasm and determination won through. Even so approval for the Sports Hall was only given after a complete revision of the original plans following a Public Planning Enquiry in 1993. By removing the Sports Hall complex to the east of the Main House and adjacent to the all weather pitch, sufficient space was freed up in the main 'building envelope' close to Park Lane to begin the modernisation of all the teaching areas.

The Cricket Pitch – School Archives

Throughout the 1990s the Head was well supported by the sterling efforts of his immediate Deputies since much of the burden of the day to day running of the School had to fall on their shoulders. Joan Spicer who retired in 1994 and Diana Hughes, who took over as Deputy Head having been Head of Science and Head of Physics for some years, did much to bring the School up to date in all its modern policies and procedures. Meanwhile Wyn James, the Second Deputy Head, worked tirelessly as the Building and Liaison Officer, linking together the thoughts and ideas of the teaching staff to the plans of the architects and the excellent work of the various contractors during construction.

Summary of the Building Development Programme

Phase 1

1995 Sports complex adjacent to the all weather pitch of 1988 was completed.

Phase 2

1996 New Cricket Pavilion completed to the south of the main 1st XI square.

1997 Refurbishment of the Sixth Form Centre in the old Stable Block.

1998 The new Art & Design Centre completed.

1999 The new Science & Technology Centre incorporating 11 laboratories and 4 workshops opened.

2000 A new Senior School classroom centre incorporating 23 teaching rooms, multimedia facilities, Senior staff offices, Staff Common Room and a modern well equipped library was opened. This was named The Haywood Centre following a staff proposal.

Phase 3

2001 The Ferndale Theatre, a studio theatre with seating for 175 people and equipped with exceptional sound and lighting facilities was opened.

2002 Extensive landscaping incorporating a new Adventure Playground for the Junior School, new hard court areas and adjacent car parks to the south of the Junior School with an extension to the Old Freemen's Clubhouse car park were all completed.

2003 The all weather pitch, which had been in use for 15 years, was replaced by a modern surface with new flood-lighting; the swimming pool which was almost 30 years old was completely refurbished and reduced in depth at the deep end; a further multimedia centre was added in the old Stable Block.

All of the above projects were made possible by the capital funding provided by the Corporation of London. The School enjoyed much assistance from the Technical Services Department at Guildhall. The clean architectural lines of the newly built areas blended wonderfully well with the older buildings on site thereby realising David Haywood's vision of a modern well integrated and superbly equipped campus.

Changes

As the country saw the introduction of the National Curriculum early in the decade, the Central Committee at School was considering other important matters – the introduction of long trousers for the Junior Boys, the installation of a bottle bank in the School grounds and the introduction of soft toilet tissue. The School also asked the Corporation to consider lowering the entry age to seven years old, to fit in with Surrey LEA changes. In 1994 a new quadrangle was added to the rear of Kemp House, extending the Junior School complex. It included three new classrooms for 7 year olds and suitable resource areas for storage as well as extra cloakooms and lockers.

The Old Freemen's Association

For the first time the Old Freemen's Association had a second member of a family acting as Chairman. Steven 'Harry' Jenkins was elected in 1990, following his mother Pat. No rugby, hockey or cricket was available in the Park owing to pitch renovation in that year. The takings at the bar showed a dramatic decline in consequence. The Old Freemen's Rugby Football Club held their first overseas tour, to America, accompanied by wives and girlfriends.

Magnificent quilt

A magnificent quilt made by Vivien Shute and Jane Lethbridge was contributed as a fund-raising raffle prize for the FSA May Fayre, 1990. Made in a traditional feathered star pattern for a five-foot bed, everyone hoped it would raise hundreds of pounds towards the funds. As raffle draw approached, the two quilters showed definite signs of reluctance about parting with their work of art. It isn't known who won it, but the profit from the Fayre was a record £7,500.

The first lady Chairman of the Governors

Lady Ponsonby became the first female Chairman of the Governors in 1992. One of her first tasks was to host the Livery lunch. She also officiated at an Old Freemen's tree planting ceremony, when the dedication had to take place in the Memorial Clubhouse owing to the rain.

Sport

With the two new grass hockey pitches in front of Main House, more matches and practice were possible. Soon nine girls from the School were playing hockey for Surrey. Cricket also benefited as the FSA purchased the School's first bowling machine for use in the nets.

Overseas tours became a feature and included the first girls' Hockey trip to Bermuda and a boys' Rugby trip to Australia and Fiji. Synchronised swimming became very popular during the 90s and was a spectacle well worth watching under the guidance of tutor Denise Tapping (née Green).

The Quilt – "Ashteadian" 115

Synchronised Swim – John Keeling

Tree planting and memorials

On the 16th June 1991, the Old Freemen had a ceremonial planting of small leafed lime trees in memory of former teachers 'Bob' Roberts (taught at the School 1909-1948) and Wallie King (taught from1932-1973). A third is in memory of Iris Cole (1918) an ex-pupil and founder member of The Old Freemen's Association. They stand along the drive up from Rookery Hill on the opposite side from the Clubhouse.

In 1996, the OFA planted two more trees and donated two benches as tributes to former staff members. One tree was for Mary Rowland and the other for John Lansdown. The two benches were dedicated to Edgar Burkes and Tom Conway.

At the same time, Keith Hood donated an attractive clock, now above the Memorial Clubhouse, and dedicated it to the memory of his brother Trevor, who died in a flying accident. He felt his brother would have wanted rugby spectators to be able to keep a check on the time.

In 1997 it was the turn of that long serving Headmaster, W.W. Parkinson (1914–1945) to have a bench dedicated to his memory. And in 1998 a garden border was planted in front of the Clubhouse in memory of Miss Hutton and 'Tubby' Rowland.

Mr & Mrs Lewis – School Archives

George Lewis retires

George Lewis retired in 1991, having taught at the School since 1971. He was Head of Art and Design for most of his School career, but took on many other responsibilities like School rugby. He was also talented in drama, both as a performer, and singer and as a builder of stage sets. His wife Jeanne also became involved and spent hours painting scenery, as well as joining the staff as a most accomplished art teacher for a few years before they retired to their native Pembroke.

From 1973 George became Gresham Housemaster, following on from Wallie King. He developed the House spirit to such an extent that Gresham won the Cock House shield no fewer than nine times between 1973 and 1989.

The School still has a number of portraits he painted of retiring colleagues, and the pen and ink drawings he did of just about every aspect of the School.

The Romanian Orphan Appeal

Pupils, staff and parents were greatly affected by the plight of children in Romania and determined to help them. They collected enough food, medical supplies, dental equipment, clothing and toys to fill three lorries. The delivery party of ten included five members of staff. It was considered most appropriate the School was helping orphanages in Romania in view of its own foundation in Brixton.

The first towns they visited were Marghita and Suceava, where a church contact distributed goods on their behalf. They then went on to visit two orphanages. Doctors at the first orphanage, called Baby's Cradle, were delighted to receive medical supplies and food, and reported other supplies were beginning to get through. Alan Moody had visited the orphanage before and was pleased to see a definite improvement in conditions there.

Unfortunately the second orphanage, for teenagers, had deteriorated. The children were dirty and had increasing behavioural problems. However, they were delighted to see the visitors with their gifts. Before they left Romania, the party looked for an orphanage the School could 'adopt' before returning home. They chose a home for incurables, housing 200 children with mental or physical disabilities. Support for this scheme continued for a number of years, and every Friday afternoon in term time the "Freemens' Aid Commitee" are loaned the Old Freemen's Clubhouse to hold a fund raising tea and cakes sale. In the last few years the Mexico Child Link project has been supported, funding help to mentally handicapped 'street' children in Puebla, south east of Mexico City.

The Intercom

In 1992, an internal School magazine was started with the main purpose of keeping staff, pupils and parents informed about affairs. Called Intercom, it informs everyone about the wealth of activities at School, including charity work, academic and sporting achievements and lists forthcoming music or drama events. In term time it is produced monthly with submitted items of general interest as well as results, fixtures and events.

The Sports Hall

The Sports Hall was completed in 1995 accommodating a variety of uses. There are three excellent squash courts, complete with viewing balcony, in one wing. The main hall can be used for hockey, netball, basketball, badminton, football, tennis and cricket. Upstairs there is a multi-activity area, which serves as lecture or function room, aerobics studio or space for drama and choreography rehearsals. Further facilities include a kitchen, changing rooms for staff and pupils, storage areas and a large office for the sports staff. The building incidentally encourages greater use of the astroturf pitch, as it brings changing room facilities conveniently closer.

The Sports Hall – John Keeling

Jonathan Bird (1991 – 2001)

"One of my earliest memories of City of London Freemen's School was being ordered by Mr Deighton to get out our PE kit for the regimental check. From that day forward I knew that if I was going to get on at Freemen's I had to get on with Mr Deighton!

The Junior School proved to be some of the best years, where I made friends for life. School socials were something to look forward to, a chance to slow dance with the girl you fancied under the eagle eyes of the teachers who all kept a watch for anyone trying to slip out to the bike sheds! No one could pass Miss Trump.

Talent Shows always brought a crowd; the main hall would be packed to see what some of the students had prepared to try and 'wow' the audience. It was a wonderful opportunity for the more extrovert to mimic the teachers and gently (or not so gently) make fun of them. It was our one and only chance to get our own back. I particularly remember the 'Freemen's Blind Date' sketch.

A highlight not only for the Junior School, but throughout the School was the traditional City visit. Every year a new and exciting destination was chosen.

My first and probably favourite destination was the Tower of London, a chance to see the Crown Jewels and run after ravens. Tea at the Guildhall was always lush, although in the last few years it didn't quite live up to expectation, a victim of cut backs perhaps?

The hype of the Senior School lived up to expectations: I got a locker. Work got a bit harder and rugby much rougher, and that was about it. New faces from other schools made our year larger and more diverse, which was good. Personally speaking, the best thing about Senior School was the rugby, inspired by 'King of the Wing' Bill Deighton. Fred Batchelor took the forwards for training and won us over by deciding to practise line-outs rather than run sprints, a true gentleman. Fred also lives in his own time zone, as our 30 seconds flat out sprinting seemed to run well into a minute. We have the PE staff to thank for the rugby tour to South Africa, in which I personally had the time of my life, something only the City of London Freemen's School could have made so enjoyable.

The other opportunity I relished was the World Challenge Expedition to Kenya in 2000, led by the ever-adventurous Mr Cox. The trip was a unique experience and culminated in an ascent of Mount Kenya. We all grew up very quickly, learning many life skills and testing our endurance to the limit.

Since I left, in 2001, the school has changed a great deal. The new Humanities and Science blocks have promoted the School as one of the top co-educational schools in the UK.

I would like to thank all those at City of London Freemen's School who helped me to enjoy my time there so much. That includes all staff, without whom I would not have so many memories, or the encouragement and determination to follow a career in Medicine. I guess if my old junior teachers, and some of my senior ones, could see me now they would not recognise me. I was always known as a bit of a comedian and for pursuing my interests on the rugby pitch rather than in the classroom, so they would be astounded I made it to medical school. But it was not without their help and continual encouragement, tinged with exasperation at times.

I had a fantastic time at City of London Freemen's School. My decision to join the Old Freemen's Association demonstrates I do not want to let my time at Freemen's go. So I have moved on from School to the Old Freemen's Association, (sobering to be considered an Old Boy at 20!). I have signed up for 10 years of fun, camaraderie, and, of course, rugby. Seriously, I hope I find the Old Freemen's Association is as enjoyable as was my time at the School, and so far I have not been disappointed."

chapter 21

THE MILLENNIUM CELEBRATIONS AND 75 YEARS IN ASHTEAD PARK

Robin Eve (1951) was elected Chief Commoner for the year 2000. He was also a Governor for the School and President of the Old Freemen's Association. The only thing he regretted about all these responsibilities was being unable to attend the School Prize Day – unfortunately he was busy representing the Lord Mayor elsewhere at the time.

On Old Freemen's Day 2000, Robin came to the School to introduce a ceremony commemorating the founding in 1854, and the transfer to Ashtead in 1926. Former pupil Ron Everest (1928) designed and made a special plaque for the occasion, which is now in the entrance hall. As he had been at School both before and after the move to Ashtead, he was keen to make something to link the past and present. At the ceremony he recalled:

"Owing to rather tragic circumstances I was a double orphan before I entered The City of London Freemen's Orphan School at Brixton in 1919. I spent seven years of my early schooling there, followed by two years here at Ashtead.

This being the Millennium year, I thought it would be the ideal time for the 72 years of The Orphan School at Brixton to be commemorated. So with the skills I was taught at School, and in my subsequent business career, I decided I would design and manufacture a suitable plaque for this purpose, and present it to the School. In some small measure it is a return for the excellent schooling I had been given as a Foundation Scholar.

I should like to emphasise that from the existence of the old Brixton Orphan School founded in 1854 by Warren Stormes Hale came the City of London Freemen's School as we know it today."

Robin Eve and Ron Everest
Plaque Unveiling – David Harn

The Haywood Centre

July 2000 saw the completion of the new Humanities building, the Haywood Centre, so named after the staff proposed the idea to The Governors to recognise the current Headmaster's immense contribution to recent development of the school. This provided the School with new senior staff offices, computing classrooms, a multi-media teaching centre, 20 classrooms for subjects including English, Mathematics, Languages, Geography, History and RE, a splendid new Library and Learning Resource Centre, and a much improved staff common room.

2001 School Inspection

February 2001 saw the visit of the Independent Schools' Inspectorate. They gave the School a glowing report, describing it as:

'A very good school. It provides a challenging education in which all pupils are encouraged to achieve their potential across a wide-ranging curriculum. At all levels in the school, academic standards are high and very good pastoral care encourages the development of confidence and personal responsibility in a community atmosphere, which promotes respect and mutual support.'

The inspectors were impressed by:

* the high academic achievement at all levels
* the well behaved pupils
* the high quality of teaching
* the well designed premises and excellent learning resources
* the strength of pastoral care
* the strong, well-directed leadership of the Headmaster – supported by a hard working and enthusiastic senior management team
* the extra-curricular programme, especially in music, sport and drama

75 Years in Ashtead Park

On 27th February 2001 the whole School was joined by the Governors, ex-Staff, Old Freemen and parents at Guildford Cathedral, to celebrate 75 years at Ashtead Park.

As well as the formal service, there was a presentation given by a small group of sixth formers, depicting some events from the history of the School.

The Revd. Simon Austen gave the sermon. Simon is an ex-pupil and his parents are also both Old Freemen. The ex-staff included former Headmaster Michael Kemp and Helen, his wife; Pauline Taylor, his Deputy Headmistress; and an impressive array of their colleagues. The School also welcomed the Revd. Charles Stewart, Canon of Winchester Cathedral, a former member of staff.

The 75 year anniversary celebrations continued all through 2001, with at least one special event each month. The Old Freemen's Association were hosted by the Chairman, Head and Senior staff at a formal dinner in the Dining Hall during April, and the Livery Day celebration was in May.

Party in the Park Programme

Setting up Party in the Park
School Archives

One of the imaginative displays in the Flower Festival
School Archives

The Party in the Park; June 2001

The School decided to have a celebratory 'Party in the Park' on 17th June, the date of the official opening in 1926, to include the Freemen's School Association, the Old Freemen's Association and the School.

Local flower arranging clubs had set up remakable, imaginative flower arrangements throughout the School, with entrance proceeds going to charities supported by the School.

On the day, there were numerous side shows, refreshment tents and a mammoth raffle, followed by an entertaining evening of dance, drama and poetry with performers recruited from past and present pupils. The finale was an ABBA Experience by Voulez Vous, followed by a spectacular firework and laser display silhouetted against the Main House.

Lime Walk in 1926 – O.F.A. Archives

Cabaret

Another major achievement of the year was the School's production of *Cabaret*. It was very favourably reviewed by a West End choreographer, Paul Dean-Lewis. He gave everyone involved an excellent report, concluding: "I hope, one day, to be able to repeat my experience of what was a most memorable evening of entertainment."

Making Echoes

The School also performed 'Making Echoes' at the Edinburgh Fringe. It was a new play adapted from the short stories of Janet Frame by Philip Tong, Head of Drama.

Julia Robertson's review in *The Scotsman* reported:
"An unspoken rule for aficionados is to avoid school productions at all costs. …considering the demands made upon the young actors by the script, the performances are first class, particularly Andrew Garfield as Mr Todd and Carina Cornwell who plays his youngest daughter, Winnie. The direction encompasses thoughtful choreography and I had to keep pinching myself to remember that this was not a professional company."

Heather Neill in the Times Educational Supplement said:
"This is a remarkable achievement for such a young cast."

The Ferndale Theatre

In October 2001 the excellent and well-designed Ferndale Theatre was opened, named after Ferndale Road in Brixton, where the original Orphan School was sited. With first class lighting and sound systems, the theatre has a 170-seat capacity. The new performing centre soon inspired pupils to use their talents to the full, and within months of opening the Theatre saw some outstanding productions and concerts.

The Chairman's Dinner

This special year included a Chairman's Dinner at Guildhall in late November with over 200 people enjoying a splendid evening. All teaching staff and partners had been invited and they joined Governors and invited guests from the FSA, OFA and many other organisations associated with the School in recent times.

The Carol Service

The closing event of the 75 year celebrations was Carols by Candlelight at St Giles' Church on December 13th. Governors, Staff, Pupils, Former Pupils and other Members of the School community attended this beautiful service.

Charles Wiard   Robin Eve   John Thorpe
Francis Paddick   Joseph Byllam Barnes
School Archives

City Connections

The School has always prided itself on its City connections. In addition to the Old Freemen on the Board of Governors, Robin Eve and Joe Byllam-Barnes, our alumni include four Past Masters of Livery Companies, John Thorpe (1946), Francis Paddick (1942), Joe Byllam-Barnes (1944) and the late Charles Wiard (1927). Robin Eve is also a former Chief Commoner.

Joseph Byllam-Barnes is a past Master of the Worshipful Company of Upholders (1993-4), a past Master of the Guild of Freemen (2000-2001), former President of the United Wards Club and a Liveryman of the Fletchers' Company. He was invited to join the Fletchers as one of his forbears, John de Billam, distinguished himself at the Battle of Agincourt.

Robin Eve is a former Chairman of the School Governors, a former Chief Commoner and Chairman of the City Lands and Bridges Committee. He also received the order of Merit (Commandeur de L'Ordre National du Merite) from the French President in recognition of his organisation of the Presidential visit.

Francis Paddick was a pupil at the City of London Freemen's School from 1937 to 1942, during which time he became Senior Prefect, and Captain of both Rugby and Cricket. Francis served as Chairman of the Old Freemen's Association. He became Master of the Broderers' Company in 1982–83.

John G. Thorpe was a pupil at the City of London Freemen's School from 1943 to 1946, and was apprenticed to the Glass Sellers' Company in 1950. In 1955 he became a Freeman and a Liveryman of that Company. He served as its Master in 1995–96. Meanwhile, in 1979, he had become a Liveryman of the Makers of Playing Cards' Company and served as its Master in 1990–91. John is also the Playing Card Company's archivist and wrote a book on the Company's history to celebrate the Millennium.

The late **Charles Wiard** entered the School as a Foundationer, on the death of his father in 1922. When he left in 1927, he was Victor Ludorum and had created a School Long Jump record of 20 feet 3 inches (6 metres 17cms), which stood until 1993. In 1936 Charles represented Great Britain in the 4 x 110 yards sprint relay at the Olympic Games in Berlin. Charles entered the services of the Corporation of London and his last appointment was as Director of Billingsgate Fish Market. While there, he entertained many Royal Family members and Heads of State in his offices, and always invited past students of the School to join him for a celebratory meal after obtaining their Freedom of the City.

The Record Breaker

The boy who broke Charles Wiard's Long Jump record was Andrew Slaughter. In 1993 he jumped 6 metres 52cms, and the following year jumped 7 metres, the current School record. One of the first to offer Andrew his congratulations was Charles Wiard.

Old Freemen's Association and the Freemen's School Association.

These organisations have not shown a great deal of change over the years. Past pupils are still welcomed into the Old Freemen's Association, which offers the use of the Clubhouse and bar for social and sporting events, together with regular newsletters and a copy of the Ashteadian. Organising the Old Freemen's Day annual reunion in June, it continues to provide the means and the opportunity for ex-pupils to keep in touch with one another.

The Freemen's School Association continues to raise funds to provide the School with extra equipment or to help finance projects not covered by School fees. Recent donations included a £10,000 contribution towards the multi-media infrastructure in the Ferndale Theatre (2001) and £12,000 for the new Junior Adventure Playground (2002).

Andrew Slaughter – O.F.A. Archives

chapter 22

WHERE ARE WE NOW?

Ben Weston

A pupil at the School between 1941 and 1949, Ben returned as a teacher from 1974 until his retirement in 1997. He has seen tremendous changes during this time.

"Since the time I left school in 1949, profound changes have taken place in society. The great increase in wealth and considerable shifting in social attitudes have had their effect on Freemen's.

Affluence

The enormous increase in general affluence has had profound results. Even after the War, in the 1945 to 1949 period, few people owned a car or went abroad for a holiday. Now many sixth formers own cars and frequently travel abroad without their parents.

When I was at Freemen's there were some very poor families, especially among the Foundationers. I would guess most parents were small businessmen, minor professionals, Civil Servants or similar.

By the time I started teaching there in 1974, and especially by my retirement in 1997, there were some very rich parents, including entrepreneurs, people in show business, leading lawyers, car dealers, photographers, TV presenters and bookmakers.

Parental involvement

I doubt if my parents visited the School more than once or twice when I was there, and they would not have known any of my teachers. At least two of my contemporaries, David Smith and Keith Hood, agree with me.

Now there are regular parents' evenings, the internal newsletter, 'Intercom' and a very active parents' association in the Freemen's School Association. I wonder if my teachers would have welcomed all this involvement?

Activities

There has been a huge increase in activities available to pupils – including overseas sporting and music trips to places as far away as South Africa, the West Indies and Australia.

Ski trips were unheard of in earlier days, while the one planned for 2004 is believed to cost in the region of £840 and will involve 88 Junior pupils. There are also expensively produced musicals, theatricals and talent shows – all involving parents' co-operation and commitment. So the parents' ability and their desire to finance their children have become important factors.

Academic achievement

There has been a great improvement in academic achievement. Most pupils today aim for high grades to get to University and many go on to enter the professions or well-paid jobs in commerce. Most of my contemporaries became clerks, or policemen, and rarely reached the highest positions. It was only the brightest few who went to University.

Staff

Staff in 1974, and particularly by my retirement in 1997, were much better qualified and had far more training than teachers when I was a pupil. There were also far more of them, to cope with the increased number of pupils. Staff are more interested in promotion or career changes today – in the 1940s they were far more likely to see their post as a job for life. (By 2003 there were over 80 teaching staff including at least 10 part time teachers; there were 840 pupils in the school, 428 boys, 412 girls. Of these 360 were in the Junior School and 192 in the Sixth Form).

I believe staff get on much better with students nowadays, and punishments are generally less rigorous. Naturally corporal punishment has been completely abolished.

Pupils

The Ferndale Theatre – John Keeling

As already mentioned, there has been a huge increase in pupils, especially in the ratio of girls to boys. When I was at school it was something like 1:5 and now there are equal numbers of girls. Also the introduction of the Junior School has meant more pupils can enter at seven years old and not leave until they are 18. When I started there was a one-form entry with a minimum age of 8 and the majority of my contemporaries left at 16.

Pupils are very much more sophisticated, probably owing to better teaching, TV, computers and foreign travel. I like to think they are much more independent, and many take off on long trips even before their Gap Year.

The Senior pupils take a much more friendly, caring attitude to the younger ones, and I feel what bullying there was has now almost ceased. Prefects have much less power than in those earlier times and this does not seem to have led to any deterioration in discipline.

The curriculum

The curriculum, like the facilities, has greatly expanded from the very limited range of subjects when I was a pupil. We were offered the three Rs, history, geography, chemistry, physics and biology with domestic science for the girls and wood or metal work for the boys.

Fees

The fees were, of course, much lower in my time and the total of 7 guineas (£7 and 7 shillings) per term for 8 years, which amounted to £176 –8 –0, would now only pay for about three or four days schooling.

Prestige

The prestige of the School has increased enormously over the years. An immense amount of money has been spent on the buildings, which has produced vastly improved facilities for teaching and other activities. In turn, this has led to improved academic, artistic, and sporting achievements. This success makes the School one of the most sought after in Surrey.

I have no doubt at all that Freemen's is a much better School now than in my time as a pupil there, when in many respects, and owing in part to war-time shortages, it was quite run down. However, I am glad that I attended the School. I have yet to discover another one that inspires the same loyalty amongst its former pupils.

The Bath Cup winners – John Keeling

The relations between the Headmaster and the staff, the staff and pupils, the parents and the school and even pupils of different ages have all changed since 1949."

Successes in 2003

The School enjoyed a year of sporting and dramatic success. In May, the senior boys' swimming team won the prestigious Bath Cup at Crystal Palace, awarded each year for the top team in the Independent Schools' National Relay Championship – not only is ours the smallest school to have won the award in 51 years but the squad also set the fifth fastest time in the Cup's history. In August, the School attracted similar acclaim with the Drama Department's special production of "Like Water For Chocolate" at the Edinburgh Fringe winning a 5-star review and being sold out for six consecutive nights. Likewise there was sell-out success story when the production came 'home' to the Ferndale Theatre, echoed some months later by the five-night run for "Les Miserables", tickets for which were sold out within hours.

A scene from Les Miserables

David Haywood

The Headmaster was asked to address the questions "So where do we stand now and what prospects for the future?" Without wishing to set an agenda for any successors, he offered the following thoughts:

"In our sesquicentenary year we can celebrate the high academic standing of the School, both locally and nationally. In November 2003 'The Independent' newspaper published its national performance tables, including the "Top 100" UK schools based on the 2003 Advanced Level point scores. CLFS was 38th nationally, so clearly promotion to the 'First Division' has been achieved and consolidated by a consistently similar performance over the last 3 years.

The very positive Inspection Report from the Independent School's Inspectorate (17 inspectors in the School for 4 days) in February 2001 was anticipated by the earlier inclusion of the School for the first time in "The Good Schools' Guide" in 2000. This is the most popular, widely read and prestigious guide to the nation's top schools and the comments on CLFS included the following:

The academic results are really good.

The School has an enviable location set in 57 acres of woodland and playing fields.

The results of the Corporation of London's funding of some £25M (at today's prices) in the last decade are modern, attractive and extremely impressive buildings.

There is a strong pastoral care system in place.

The description of the School concluded thus:

A very attractive school that offers outstanding facilities and opportunities for all its pupils. Egalitarian in feel, it is not the place for social climbers. The sort of school that makes one believe in the benefits of co-education.

Despite the excellence of all the modern facilities and systems, there is still much to be done to improve the School. The Inspection Report in 2001 referred to the need to give consideration to improving the facilities for dining, for boarding

David Haywood, current Headmaster – John Keeling

Art and Design Centre (1998) – John Keeling

and for Music. A current accommodation review is thus examining the options for better dining and music provision and for the future of boarding; now less that 10% of Senior School pupils are regular boarders i.e. 35-40 pupils. Most come from overseas, but financial considerations indicate that boarding is not a significant drain on school resources despite the relatively low numbers.

So again it is time for Freemen's to be bold and innovative. It is necessary to refuse the easy trappings of the comfort zone, just as it has throughout its history. It would have been easier for the Committee to close the orphan school in Brixton rather than take the bold decision to move elsewhere in 1926. Similarly, in the post-war period after some 25 years at Ashtead, faced with increased competition from the expanded grammar schools, the easy way would have been decline and closure. In 1954 the School's Centenary was marked by the 50th edition of the Ashteadian, which reported a school roll of only 241 pupils. Eric Fielden, the Headmaster, in his Prize Day Report commented that the roll was at its lowest for some time. But bold development with new buildings in the next two decades brought steady expansion and progress. Michael Kemp's vision then initiated the Junior School plans some 20 years ago, when alternative options may have promoted stagnation and decline in a highly competitive market place. Latterly, we have rebuilt the whole Senior School with the bold implementation of a comprehensive re-development and landscaping programme of imaginative expansion, backed by the welcome and invaluable financial resources of the Corporation. As the School is now doing so well, it is undoubtedly the very time not to sit back but to forge ahead and to make the most of an outstanding location, backed by a nationally acclaimed reputation, to secure the future of this exceptional School for another 150 years."

The Science block (1998) – John Keeling

Alexandra Boag (Head Girl 2002-2003)

"As I look back over my time at Freemen's, I am filled with great warmth and admiration for the School and the people who so successfully run it. And as I consider just how immensely lucky I have been to spend ten of the most important years at Freemen's, I try to pinpoint just exactly what it is that makes the School the huge triumph it is today.

Even just looking back over the past ten years, the physical changes to the School structure are vast - but when we look back to 150 years ago, they are just colossal! However, there is one underlying factor that has remained unchanged in the School's make up, and that is its unfaltering devotion to the development and achievement of the many pupils who leave Freemen's each year.

The opportunities to develop and grow as an individual are endless. Whether you are a musician, an academic, sportsman, or indeed a comedian - there is always an aspect of Freemen's that allows each and every individual to have...

...their moment to shine."

"The School has an enviable location set in 57 acres of woodland and playing fields." ISI Inspection Report 2001 – *John Keeling*

bibliography and thanks

Bibliography

Ashteadians

City of London Freemen's School 1854-1954

Sheep over London Bridge Caroline Arnold

Discovering London's Guilds and Liveries John Kennedy Melling

Illustrated English Social History 4 GM Trevelyan

The Freedom of the City of London Guidhall Library

Acknowledgements

My thanks to those who have loaned or given photographs, and to the School Maintenance Officer, Tony Riley, who has produced photographs under the most challenging demands, such as lifting individuals from a group scene. Tim Cox who supported my efforts with every item of news or picture he could find. His wife, Cecilia, was a great help with a number of the graphics and the School archives will benefit from her reproductions. I would also like to thank Martin Hearne who did a marvellous job of proof reading my original draft, and all those pupils and members of staff, both past and present, who took time to send me their memories of the School.

My apologies to anyone who feels that their time at the School has not been fully recognised. I was largely dependent on former pupils' recollections and not all the periods were covered.

Patricia Jenkins May 2004

index

Montague	RE	Headmaster	22,25,35
Mortimer	Dr	Headmaster	12,16
Paddick	F	Pupil	135,136
Panton	Della	Pupil	115,116
Parkinson	WW	Headmaster	1,35,39,41,42,60,67
			68,69,75,81,83,91,93,94
Patterson nee Mills 74		Evelyn	Pupil
Payne	Alan	Pupil	74
Pettman	John	Pupil	71,74
Pike	Mrs	Matron	12
Pittom	Kate nee Little	Pupil	94
Ponsnoby	Lady	Chairman of Governors	127
Richards	Edward	Pupil	3
Roberts	ER	Master	25,42,60,68,71,93,94,128
Robins	Miss	Mistress	25,30,42,43,51,84,93
Robertshawe	Miss R	Mistress	93
Rowland	BE	Master	75,76,78,94,99,111,112
Rowland	Mary	Mistress	69,76,78,81,128
Sears	Mrs	Mistress	105
Selwood	Samuel	Porter	12
Shurmer	Russell	Pupil	89
Sissons	Major	Master	74
Slaughter	Andrew	Pupil	136
Smith	Miss	Mistress	13
Smith	Rev Brownrigg	Headmaster	13,16,21,93
Smith	Harold Victor	Pupil	27
Somers nee Watling 107		Beatrice	Pupil
Sparks	Miss	Mistress	44
Spicer	Joan	Mistress	125
Stephenson	Mr	Master	22
Steptoe	Mr	Master	103
Stilwell	Michael	Bursar	117